Hilda Hughes.

From the Romney portrait

BURKE'S

SPEECH ON CONCILIATION

WITH AMERICA

EDITED
WITH NOTES AND AN INTRODUCTION

BY

HAMMOND LAMONT

FORMERLY PROFESSOR OF RHETORIC IN
BROWN UNIVERSITY

GINN AND COMPANY

BOSTON · NEW YORK · CHICAGO · LONDON
ATLANTA · DALLAS · COLUMBUS · SAN FRANCISCO

The Athenæum Press

GINN AND COMPANY · PRO-
PRIETORS · BOSTON · U.S.A.

TO MY FATHER

THOMAS LAMONT

PREFACE.

———◦◦◦———

THE object of this volume is to present in compact form all the material needed by teacher or student for a complete understanding of Burke's greatest speech, that on *Conciliation with America.*

The text, except for modernized capitalization, spelling and punctuation, and the correction of a few typographical errors, follows a copy of the First Edition, London, 1775.

The Introduction contains no newly discovered facts, but simply attempts to show how those already known in regard to the condition of Great Britain, the relations between the mother country and her colonies, Burke's career, his principles and his style, bear upon the subject-matter and the form of this speech. It also supplies references to the proper authorities on matters concerning which the student may desire fuller details.

The Notes indicate some of the sources from which Burke drew elements in his style, mark the similarity in ideas and expression between this speech and his other writings, and explain, not only obscurities, but the many allusions which appealed to his hearers but which are partly or wholly lost on modern readers. The notes referring to Greek and Latin

authors, to the Bible and to English poets for passages which
have been quoted by Burke, or which seem to have affected
his thought or style, were mostly collected by C. A. Goodrich,
in his *Select British Eloquence*, and by E. J. Payne, Burke's
Select Works, Clarendon Press, 1892, vol. I; they have
appeared in several subsequent editions, and the substance of
the more important is here reprinted without further acknowledgment. The definitions of obsolete or peculiar words and
the explanations of parliamentary usages have been handed
down from Goodrich, with more or less addition at each transmission; but they have been treated with special fulness by
F. G. Selby, Burke's *Speeches*, Macmillan, New York, 1895.
Some of the parallel passages from Burke himself have also
been pointed out by Payne, Selby or Professor A. S. Cook,
Speech on Conciliation, Longmans, New York, 1896; but the
great majority of them are new in this edition. The most
important notes are those which throw light on Burke's inferences from the events which had already estranged England and
her colonies; on his manner of summing up everything said on
all sides during ten years of discussion of American affairs; on
the political or personal bearing of many remarks which we
might deem insignificant; on his dexterity in turning against
his opponents their own phrases, convicting them out of their
own mouths; in short, on the force of this speech as an argument. Notes of this kind, in so far as they are needed to
elucidate matters which Burke directly mentions, are given in
most editions. Some of the allusions, however, are difficult to
trace, owing to the fragmentary state even of the completest
reports of parliamentary proceedings, and but few actually were

traced until Professor Cook gathered from such valuable but obvious sources as the *Parliamentary History*, the *Annual Register* and the histories of Bancroft and Lecky a considerable body of material relating to the debates on America. Of such notes some in this volume are specially credited to him ; some are substantially identical with his, because the present editor, before seeing Professor Cook's edition, made a systematic study of the same sources ; and many are now published for the first time.

For helpful suggestions the thanks of the editor are due Professor John Matthews Manly of Brown University.

H. L.

PROVIDENCE, R. I.,
    May 13, 1897.

TABLE OF CONTENTS.

INTRODUCTION.

I.

ACQUAINTANCE WITH BURKE.

"I MUST be in a wretched state indeed when your company would not be a delight to me."[1] These words, which the dying Dr. Johnson addressed to Edmund Burke, can be sincerely repeated even now by any one who really gets acquainted with him. Without some acquaintance, however, with Burke himself and with his environment, one may fail to realize that, far from being a mere eloquent declaimer about matters settled a hundred years before we were born, he is rather the greatest of statesmen, discussing the very problems which vex us to-day. To understand him wholly, even in the *Speech on Conciliation with America*, one must have a considerable knowledge of the social conditions in his time, of the political situation, of his character, his principles of statecraft and his style.

II.

SOCIAL CONDITIONS.

The social conditions of England in Burke's day are most fully laid before us in the clear-cut pictures of Boswell's *Life of Johnson*, Horace Walpole's *Letters*, Madame D'Arblay's *Diary*

[1] Boswell's *Life of Johnson*, edited by G. Birkbeck Hill, Oxford, 1887, IV, 407.

and Letters and Jesse's *George Selwyn and His Contemporaries.*[1]
In these works such small details as tie-wigs and swords,
journeys from country to town by coach and four, pleasure
parties at Vauxhall Gardens, dinners of the Literary Club at
the Turk's Head, gossip about the shameless old Marquis of
Queensberry and tears over the woes of Clarissa Harlowe
often show the real temper of the age more distinctly than do
the generalizations of formal history.   Halfway between gossip
and history come Thackeray's entertaining lectures on George
the Second and George the Third in the *Four Georges*, and on
Hogarth, Smollett, Fielding, Sterne and Goldsmith in the
English Humorists.   Leslie Stephen's *History of English
Thought in the Eighteenth Century* treats more particularly the
intellectual side of life.[2] Of the regular histories, Lecky's *England in the Eighteenth Century*[3] goes over the whole ground
minutely, and Green's *History of the English People*[4] focusses
the same wide view into small space.   All these books exhibit
the first stage of the transformation from the slow, insular,
unorganized country seen in the writings of Dryden and Pope,
Addison, Steele and Swift, to the quickly moving, cosmopolitan,
highly organized modern England.

One important element in the development was the broader
diffusion of intelligence.   It is true that the wits still gathered
in the London coffee-houses, and, as Dr. Johnson and David
Garrick had done, men still came to town to make fortunes in
business and attain eminence in all professions ; but life out-
side London was becoming a bit less dull.   Owing in part to
the popularity which the *Tatler* and the *Spectator* had given to
periodical literature, newspapers were springing up in all the
cities and leading towns, and were carrying into every village
the discussion of such topics as the social theories of Rousseau,
Dr. Smollett's new novel *Humphrey Clinker*, and the last letter

---

[1] London, 1843.   [3] New York, 1878-90, VI, 138-300.
[2] See chapter xii.   [4] New York, 1880, IV, 206-210, 272-283.

of Junius in the *Public Advertiser.* More or less complete reports of the proceedings of Parliament bore the voices of Fox, Pitt and Burke[1] to an audience consisting of the whole nation.

Another element on which both Green and Lecky[2] lay much stress was the so-called Methodist movement. Though the followers of Wesley and Whitfield were ridiculed[3] as fanatics or snivelling hypocrites, nevertheless before the middle of the century their zeal had gone beyond the narrow limits of the sect, and was deepening the moral earnestness of all England. This fresh impulse toward cleaner thinking and living was shaming the coarseness and profligacy of the age of Anne, as revealed in the brutal pages of Swift, and was driving out the cynical corruption of Sir Robert Walpole's day, when every man had his price and even a clergyman would buy a bishopric from a king's mistress.[4] Above all, it was steadily strengthening that interest in philanthropy now so widespread. It stirred not only individual leaders like John Howard, but Parliament[5] and various local governing boards as well, to discuss plans for ameliorating the condition of the poor, the sick, the imprisoned and the enslaved. Indeed it had already gained for the anti-slavery movement such parliamentary support[6] that Burke's references to the "inhuman traffic"[7] must have quickened his hearers' attention, just as any mention of aid for the unemployed quickens ours.

The most noteworthy change of all, however, was the expansion of commerce. Burke tells how foreign trade had shot up;[8] no less remarkable had been the increase in domestic.

---

[1] The *Speech on Conciliation* was issued in pamphlet soon after delivery.

[2] II, 568–699.

[3] See Anstey's *New Bath Guide*, published in 1766.

[4] Thackeray's *George the Second*, London, 1869, 46.

[5] See *Parliamentary History*, London, 1806–20, XVII, 639–643, 843–848

[6] Lecky, VI, 279–281.

[7] See 32 22. [8] Pages 11–13.

Mines of coal, iron and tin were opening, factories and furnaces were multiplying, and canals were building which made possible a volume of internal traffic never before dreamed of. This development of business at home and abroad had affected every class in the community, but had thrust the mercantile class into special prominence; it had bestowed on the newly rich an influence[1] hitherto reserved as a sort of prerogative of the aristocracy. It had enabled merchants, or those anxious to guard mercantile interests, to play a more important part in Parliament[2] than ever before, and in debates over taxes, treaties, war and peace, to demand decisions favorable to English industries. This it was that gave to Burke's arguments[3] for the commercial advantages of conciliation the greatest weight both with Parliament and the nation at large.

III.

POLITICAL CONDITIONS.

The course of events leading up to this speech is related in all English or American histories that deal with the period.[4]

[1] See Burke's Speech on the *Nabob of Arcot's Debts, Works,* Boston, 1894, III, 24, 25.

[2] See *Parliamentary History,* XVI, 133–135; XVIII, 168, 184, 219, 461.

[3] See pages 11–13, 30, 31, 39, 40, 66, 67, 69–72.

[4] Detailed accounts may be found in Lecky and in Bancroft, *History of the United States,* New York, 1888, from II, 319, to IV, 120; more condensed narratives in Green, Andrews's *History of the United States,* New York, 1894, period iii, chs. i–iv, Goldwin Smith's *United States,* New York, 1893, ch. ii, and Fiske's *American Revolution,* Boston, 1891, chs. i, ii, and the first part of iii; and yet briefer summaries in the introductions to Selby's edition of Burke's *Speeches,* New York, 1895, and Morley's edition in the *Universal Library,* London, 1892. Bancroft's relation of proceedings in Parliament must be taken with some allowance; for even when his authority seems to have been the *Parliamentary History,* he now and then omits qualifying clauses from speeches, and thus makes men appear more hostile to America than they actually were.

According to all authorities,[1] though England and her colonies had not been actually hostile during the first half of the eighteenth century, nevertheless several causes were producing irritation on both sides. In the first place, the mother country, by a short-sighted effort to keep a monopoly of commerce and manufactures, had from time to time laid restrictions upon them.[2] Such were the laws that the colonists must export and import only in English or American vessels ; that they must trade only with England and her colonies ; that they must not erect mills for rolling and slitting iron ; and that they must not export hats. To these vexations, which in view of the growth in colonial population and industries were by no means inconsiderable, she had, through the sheer tactlessness of her agents, added many annoyances in methods of administration. Her executive officers, from governors down, were inclined to exert their powers to the extreme and even beyond legal limits. They occasionally suspended the writ of *habeas corpus*, interfered with the freedom of the press, and attempted to deprive towns of representation in the legislature.[3] The people, on their part, proud of their English blood and their English liberties, protested in town-meetings and legislative assemblies, and often treated the king's officers with scant respect, sometimes with violence. Then while the colonists waxed more and more indignant, England was inevitably led by the reports of her agents into harsher severities ; for she fully believed the Americans to be a discontented, hot-tempered, lawless crowd,[4] sorely in need of strong government.

[1] The succeeding outline is drawn from all the authorities mentioned in the preceding note, and from the *Parliamentary History*, Dodsley's *Annual Register*, *Journals of the American Congress*, *Letters* of Junius, and Adolphus's *History of England from the Accession to the Decease of George the Third*, London, 1840–45, but Fiske is followed most closely.

[2] See 39 10, note.

[3] Fiske, I, 3.

[4] 33 11, note ; also Adolphus, II, 102, 103.

The ill feeling was further inflamed by the attitude of the king himself. When George the Third came to the throne in 1760, he found his authority scarcely more than nominal; for upon the expulsion of James the Second in 1688, the Tories had sullenly left the government to the Whigs, and the latter so distrusted royal power that they had reduced it to the narrowest limits. George, however, was determined not to be a puppet in the hands of his ministers. Dull, industrious, stubborn, he was resolved that on both sides of the Atlantic he would rule in fact as well as in name.

Unhappily for England, he met with ineffectual resistance, because his supporters were united and his enemies divided. He was firmly backed by the Tories, who had begun to emerge from retirement, and who found in him a sovereign exactly to their tastes, a believer in the divine right of kings. He was unsteadily opposed by the disunited Whigs. Of the several factions he had less to fear from the Conservatives, or Old Whigs; for they were not only split, but they were so content with the state of things under which England and their party had thriven that they were averse to radical reforms. On the other hand, the king dreaded and hated the New Whigs under the lead of the elder Pitt; for they were fighting with considerable unanimity and zeal for the enlargement of popular influence through more complete representation. They complained that Parliament no longer reflected public opinion, because cities like Birmingham and Leeds, which had recently become important, were without representation, while ancient boroughs which had dwindled into insignificance had seats which were openly bought and sold, or else were under the control of a few Old Whig families. With the help of the Tories headed by Lord North, George played one faction against the other. He strove to break the power of the Old Whigs by getting their "rotten boroughs" into his own hands, and he weakened the New Whigs by the use of political patronage. Thus he kept each too feeble to block him.

With England and America both irritated, with the king bent on stretching his authority, and with opposition to him shattered by faction, events moved swiftly to a crisis. In 1763 George Grenville became Prime Minister, and Charles Townshend First Lord of Trade, that is, head of the committee of the Privy Council in charge of colonial affairs. Both were royal henchmen. Townshend believed in holding the colonies with a firm hand, in depriving them of the right of self-government, and in maintaining authority by a standing army supported by taxes assessed on the Americans by Parliament. To such lengths Grenville was unwilling to go, but he was ready to lay a tax in order to defray the expenses of the French and Indian War which had closed in 1763, — to lay a tax in spite of the fact, fully acknowledged by Parliament,[1] that the colonists had already borne more than their share of the burden. For carrying out his purpose he introduced into the Commons in 1764 a resolution[2] asserting the propriety of raising an American revenue by requiring stamps on all legal documents. He soon heard protests,[3] however, from the assemblies of Massachusetts, Connecticut, New York, Pennsylvania, Virginia and South Carolina. These bodies held that Parliament had no right to tax the colonies without their consent, but declared that in response to a request from the king the colonies would contribute, according to their means, to the needs of the British Empire. Notwithstanding these remonstrances, Grenville got his Stamp Act passed in 1765. America was furious. In October a congress of delegates from Massachusetts, Rhode Island, Connecticut, New York, New Jersey, Pennsylvania, Delaware, Maryland and South Carolina met at New York and framed formal protests; merchants agreed to import no more goods from England ; in some colonies the people threw

---

[1] See page 55.
[2] *Parliamentary History*, XV, 1427.
[3] Fiske, I, 16, 17.

the boxes of stamps into the sea; in most they compelled the stamp officers to resign; and in Massachusetts a mob sacked the house of Chief Justice Hutchinson.

At this juncture Lord Rockingham, leader of that faction of the Old Whigs with which Burke usually acted, became Prime Minister, and proposed the repeal of the Stamp Act on the ground of policy. During the hot debates over this motion and over all subsequent proceedings in regard to America, the "king's friends" [1] were firm against the colonies, because defeat for the royal plan for America might mean defeat for it in England. They argued that the colonists were actuated by nothing but the rankest ingratitude and a sordid wish to get the protection of England without paying for it, [2] and that — as Burke phrases the idea — the "right of taxation is necessarily involved in the general principle of legislation." [3] To this view Pitt and his adherents were violently opposed, for they understood that the cause of America was exactly the same as that for which they were fighting in England. [4] They maintained that representation is a natural right. [5] Between these two extremes the Rockingham Whigs steered a middle course. They held that even if Parliament had a right to tax the colonies, the exercise of it was the height of folly. [6] Finally, in 1766, the Rockingham ministry, with the help of New Whigs, carried the repeal, and at the same time, with the help of Tories, a Declaratory Act, asserting the power to make

---

[1] See 17 8, note.

[2] See speech of George Grenville, Jan. 14, 1766, *Parliamentary History*, XVI, 101, 102.

[3] See 37 11, 12; also the speech of Grenville, above.

[4] See speech of Colonel Barré, Jan. 26, 1775, *Parliamentary History*, XVIII, 191.

[5] See 37 6–10; the speech of Pitt, Jan. 14, 1766, *Parliamentary History*, XVI, 97–101; his speech May 27, 1774, XVII, 1353–1356; and the speech of Governor Johnstone, Feb. 6, 1775, XVIII, 253–262.

[6] See 37 23–38 3, and 57 16–18.

laws for the colonies "in all cases whatsoever." [1]   The repeal so pleased the people of London that in the streets they cheered Pitt and hissed Grenville.   It so pleased the Americans that they kindled bonfires, and, regarding the Declaratory Act as a mere empty form, voted addresses of thanks and loyalty.

No sooner was England out of this scrape than she blundered into another.   In a few months the Rockingham ministry was succeeded by the Grafton ministry, in which Townshend was the leading spirit.   In accordance with his own views and those of the king, he brought in a bill to lay duties on wine, oil and fruits carried directly to America from Spain and Portugal, and on glass, paper, lead, painters' colors and tea. [2] The resulting revenue he proposed to use for the salaries of royal governors, justices appointed at the king's pleasure, and civil officers responsible only to the crown, [3] — a blow at the principle of self-government, as regards both taxation and the control of officers.   The purpose of George the Third was even more nakedly set forth when Parliament suspended the assembly of New York for refusal to provide certain supplies for the army. [4]   It is true that in 1769 Parliament repealed all the duties except that on tea, but England had let the time slip by for conciliating America by a partial surrender.

During the next six years the efforts of England to compel submission made the resistance of the colonies only the more stubborn.   When revenue officers enforced the laws with rigor and intolerable insolence, merchants renewed their agreements not to import English goods, and women pledged themselves to wear homespun clothes and abstain from tea.   When in Rhode Island the captain of the revenue schooner "Gaspee"

---

[1] *Parliamentary History*, XVI, 177.
[2] See 36 4, note.
[3] *Parliamentary History*, XVI, 375, 376.
[4] *Ibid.*, 331–341.

made illegal seizures and stole hogs and sheep from the farmers, they retaliated by burning his vessel. When John Hancock's sloop "Liberty" was seized in Boston, a riot broke out. When England sent troops to overawe the inhabitants, the latter refused to provide quarters. When the soldiers irritated the populace, another riot resulted. In 1772 the king attempted to control the judiciary by ordering that all Massachusetts judges holding office during his pleasure should be paid by the crown: the colonists, unable to obtain redress through the regular government, organized committees of correspondence which bound the whole country together in common action.[1] The next year, in the hope of driving the Americans to buy tea, England despatched shiploads of it to Boston, New York, Philadelphia and Charleston: the committees of correspondence decided that the cargoes must go back. The governor of Massachusetts would not issue clearance papers for a return: the people of Boston threw the tea into the harbor. Thereupon Parliament, spurred on by the king, proceeded to measures yet more vigorous. It closed the port of Boston;[2] practically annulled the charter of Massachusetts;[3] ordered that soldiers or revenue officers indicted for murder in Massachusetts should be tried in Great Britain;[4] provided for the quartering of troops;[5] and extended the boundaries of Canada to the Ohio River[6] in defiance of the claims which Massachusetts, Connecticut, New York and Virginia laid to the territory. By this last law, known as the Quebec Act, England managed also to offend deeply both the religious and the political prejudices of the colonists;[7] for the act sanctioned Roman Catholicism throughout Canada, and established a

---

[1] Fiske, I, 78–80.
[2] See 36 4, note.
[3] See 27 18, note.
[4] See 36 4, note.
[5] *Parliamentary History*, XVII, 1353–1356.
[6] *Ibid.*, 1357–1400, 1402–1406.
[7] *Journals of Congress*, I, 22, 23, 30, 37, 40–45, 47.

government recognizing neither trial by jury nor *habeas corpus* nor popular meetings.   To enforce the first three of these laws the government stationed General Gage at Boston with more troops. Although England had aimed most of this hostile legislation especially at Massachusetts, she had struck all the colonies so hard that they instantly forgot local jealousies, and made the cause of the sufferer their own.   When the royal governors dissolved the provincial assemblies for expressing sympathy,[1] the colonies united in the Congress at Philadelphia in the autumn of 1774.   This body heartily supported Massachusetts ;[2] it asserted the freedom of the provincial legislatures "in all cases of taxation and internal polity";[3] it demanded the repeal of the obnoxious acts of Parliament ;[4] it formed an agreement to stop trade with Great Britain, Ireland and the British West Indies ;[5] and it issued addresses to the people of Great Britain,[6] to the colonists,[7] to the inhabitants of Quebec,[8] and to the king.[9]   When in reply Parliament declared a rebellion [10] and proposed further restraints upon the New England commerce and fisheries,[11] America hastened her preparations for war.

IV.

EDMUND BURKE.

In this long struggle between the king and his subjects, Burke, though by temperament a conservative, was on the side

---

[1] See letter of General Gage from Salem, June 26, 1774, *Parliamentary History*, XVIII, 85, 86 ; letter of Governor Wentworth of New Hampshire, June 8, 1774, *ibid.*, 109; and letter of Governor Dunmore of Virginia, May 29, 1774, *ibid.*, 136.

[2] *Journals of Congress*, I, 14, 17.

[3] *Ibid.*, 20, 21.

[4] *Ibid.*, 21, 22.

[5] *Ibid.*, 23, 24.

[6] *Ibid.*, 26-31.

[7] *Ibid.*, 31-38.

[8] *Ibid.*, 40-54.

[9] *Ibid.*, 46-49.

[10] See 35 23, note.

[11] See 3 8, note.

of the people.   This sympathy may be due in part to the fact
that he was a native of a country which had suffered long under
oppression.   He was born in Ireland in 1729,[1] the son of a
solicitor in good practice.   Though Burke's mother was a
Roman Catholic and brought up his sister in the same faith,
yet he and his two brothers adopted the religion of their
Protestant father.   Throughout his life, however, he was always
so tolerant of Catholics that he was sometimes charged with
being a Jesuit.

At the age of about twelve he went to school to a Quaker,
Abraham Shackleton, for whose character he had the highest
regard,[2] and to whom he always professed to owe the best part
of his education.   After two years with Mr. Shackleton, of
whose son Richard he made a lasting friend, Burke entered
Trinity College, Dublin, where he took his bachelor's degree in
1748.   In the half-dozen letters which he wrote from college
to Shackleton, he stands before us full of attraction, — a young
man brimming with life, serious in thought, and eager for
knowledge.   In some pages he gives vivacious accounts of
his walks in the country,[3] and in others he considers such
matters as the still unsettled question of the salvation of the
heathen : " I am of your opinion that those poor souls who
never had the happiness of hearing that saving name shall in
no wise be damned.   But, as you know, . . . there are several
degrees of felicity : a lower one, which the mercy of God will
suffer them to enjoy, but not anything to be compared to that
of those who have lived and died in Christ." [4]   A bishop could

---

[1] Of the several biographies of Burke the best are James Prior's, 2
vols., London, 1854; John Morley's small volume in the *English Men of
Letters*, and the twenty pages in the *Dictionary of National Biography*.   In
connection with any of them the *Correspondence*, London, 1844, is very
interesting.   Accounts of Burke's life, in some respects prejudiced, but
showing contemporary opinion, appeared in the *Annual Register* for
1797 and 1798.   The present narrative is based upon Morley's.

[2] *Correspondence*, I, 254.   [3] *Ibid.*, 4–6.   [4] *Ibid.*, 9.

not be more cocksure. In his pursuit of knowledge Burke seems to have been rather unsystematic. Of his fits of "madness" over various studies he wrote : "First I was greatly taken with natural philosophy, which, while I should have given my mind to logic, employed me incessantly. This I call my *furor mathematicus.* But this worked off as soon as I began to read it in the college, as men by repletion cast off their stomachs all they have eaten. Then I turned back to logic and metaphysics. Here I remained a good while, and with much pleasure ; and this was my *furor logicus,* a disease very common in the days of ignorance and very uncommon in these enlightened times. Next succeeded the *furor historicus,* which also had its day, but is now no more, being entirely absorbed in the *furor poeticus.*" [1] By the *furor poeticus* he was inspired to some hundred and fifty lines which have been printed in the *Correspondence,* — and no one knows how much more, — of such verse as might be expected of the average sophomore when Pope's fame was at its height. Unsystematic though Burke may have been, he nevertheless kept at work : "I spend three hours almost every day in the public library," he says.[2] "I have read some history. I am endeavoring to get a little into the accounts of this our own poor country."[3]

The seventeen years between graduation and 1765, when Burke's career was finally determined by his election to Parliament, he spent in various employments. He went to London with the intention of taking up law, but succumbed to the attractions of literature and philosophy. Prevented by ill health from steady application, he traveled considerably in England and on the Continent ;[4] he frequented debating clubs and theatres, and he did more or less hack work for the booksellers. He published nothing, however, with which his name is connected till the two books of 1756 : *A Vindication of*

---

[1] *Correspondence,* I, 22.   [3] *Ibid.,* 20.
[2] *Ibid.,* 19.   [4] *Ibid.,* 32.

Natural Society and *A Philosophical Inquiry into the Origin of our Ideas on the Sublime and Beautiful.* In the first he attempted to refute Bolingbroke's arguments against revealed religion by showing that they might be urged with equal force against the thing which in his eyes was scarcely less sacred, the social organization by which the rights of the individual are maintained. In the second book he took up a subject much discussed at the time ; and, though his speculations have been superseded, he has the credit of stimulating Lessing to the production of *Laocoon*, which is regarded as the most valuable contribution of that age to æsthetic thought.[1] Burke also wrote, or helped to write, an *Account of the European Settlements in America* and an *Abridgment of the History of England.* Then in 1759 he began to edit for Dodsley that summary of important events, the *Annual Register*, with which he was connected for thirty years. In 1761 he went to Ireland, attached in some indefinite way, perhaps as a sort of secretary, to William Gerard Hamilton, — "Single-speech" Hamilton, — who was secretary to the lord-lieutenant. Here Burke studied on the spot those evil effects of oppression on which he dwells in this speech ;[2] for the punishment of Irish rebellion by restricting commerce and manufactures, by taking many of the ordinary rights of citizens from the Catholics, who were in an enormous majority, and by confiscating land and outlawing owners,[3] had impoverished the country and rendered the people ferocious. After two years in Dublin, Burke, finding that, contrary to agreement, he must give all his time and energy to Hamilton and resign his literary ambitions, indignantly broke with his patron[4] and returned to England. There he joined

---

[1] Morley's *Burke*, 18.

[2] See pages 43–46.

[3] Green, IV, 54 ; Burke's *Tract on the Popery Laws*, *Works*, VI, 299.

[4] See *Correspondence*, I, 46–51, 55–78, 83, 84; and Augustine Birrell's *Obiter Dicta*, Second Series, New York, 1887, 165–170.

the famous Literary Club with which are associated the names of Johnson, Goldsmith, Sir Joshua Reynolds and Garrick.

In this brilliant circle Burke stood among the first. "That fellow," said Johnson, "calls forth all my powers." [1] In recognition of his general abilities and of the knowledge of politics which he had shown in the *Annual Register*, he was offered the post of private secretary to Lord Rockingham when the latter became Prime Minister in 1765. This place Burke accepted, and just at the close of the year he was elected a member of Parliament from Wendover. Within a week or two after taking his seat, at the beginning of 1766, he had spoken twice for the repeal of the Stamp Act. That he produced a strong impression is evident from one of Dr. Johnson's letters : "He has gained more reputation than perhaps any man at his [first] appearance ever gained before. He made two speeches in the House for repealing the Stamp Act which were publicly commended by Mr. Pitt, and have filled the town with wonder." [2] Upon the fall of the Rockingham ministry, Burke, who might have had a place under the new administration, remained with his friends. Turning to their account his literary powers, he began his series of great political tracts which have outlived so much other writing of the kind, because he treats of passing events in the light of enduring wisdom. First in 1769 he put forth the *Observations on the Present State of the Nation*, a reply to a pamphlet by George Grenville, who had accused his successors of ruining the country. In this controversy Burke showed himself a master of the intricate details of revenue and finance.

At this point in his career he took part in some transactions which gave his enemies a handle against him. Though he had been living almost from hand to mouth till he entered Parliament, he bought in 1768 an estate worth upwards of one hundred thousand dollars in our money, and correspondingly expensive to maintain. The matter has been much discussed

---

[1] Boswell's *Life of Johnson*, II, 450.　　[2] *Ibid.*, 16.

by biographers and critics, but has never been settled with complete satisfaction. This much, however, is clear : Burke lived on terms of close intimacy with his brother Richard and a distant kinsman, William Burke. Richard and William, together with Lord Verney, a political patron of Edmund, speculated wildly in stock of the East India Company, and later Richard was engaged in some questionable dealings in West Indian lands. That these ventures were shared by Burke has been charged but never proved. In vindication of his conduct it can be shown that most of the money for the purchase of his estate, Beaconsfield, he raised on a mortgage and on his bond to Lord Rockingham. After getting the place, he was so straitened for means to keep it up that he borrowed right and left from his friends. For example, he was in debt thirty thousand pounds to Lord Rockingham at the death of the latter in 1782, and Rockingham directed that the debt should be cancelled in view of Burke's faithful services. From these facts and others it appears that Burke's faults were neither dishonesty in speculation nor venality in Parliament, but rather a desire to live as he thought became a man in high position, a free-handed carelessness and improvidence which led him to lend or give even more readily than he borrowed or accepted, and an adherence to eighteenth-century standards of propriety, which in such things were lower than ours.

Whatever may have been his shortcomings in these private affairs, his public services outweigh them a thousand times. For one thing, he was on the right side in the long contest over Wilkes. This man, a radical writer who had been outlawed for libel, was in 1768 elected to Parliament from the county of Middlesex. Parliament, subservient to the king, expelled him. Then he was returned three times in quick succession, and each time the House pronounced his election void.[1] Having

---

[1] Green, IV, 243–247. *Parliamentary History*, XVI, 532–596. The case forms the basis of many of the attacks of Junius upon the government.

by this action wrought the people up to the pitch of rioting, the government, in order to quell disturbances, called out a military force which killed some twenty people.   When the question of excluding Wilkes was pending, Burke in several speeches defended the right of a constituency to elect whom it pleases. The dispute, he said, was not "between the House and the freeholders of Middlesex, but between the House and all the voters in England, who would easily perceive their franchises invaded." [1]   The matter of the riot Burke also brought before the House in a motion for a committee of inquiry.   In the debate he declared: "When this House shall be found . . . ready to punish the excesses of the people, and slow to listen to their grievances; . . . ready to entertain notions of the military power as incorporated with the Constitution,[2] . . . then the House of Commons will change that character which it receives from the people only." [3]

Since these sentiments were, in general, those of the *Letters* of Junius, and since Burke was known to be one of the most powerful writers of the day, he was by many suspected of being Junius.   This accusation, however, he denied,[4] and when he published his *Thoughts on the Cause of the Present Discontents* in 1770, he presented convincing evidence to all doubters.   For aside from differences of opinion between the *Letters* and the *Thoughts*, Burke did not use as his weapon the railing and invective of Junius, but argument.   In this pamphlet Burke reviewed the whole policy which led to the outbreak.   He showed how the king and his small knot of secret advisers were building up authority for themselves.[5]   He argued that the powers

[1] *Parliamentary History*, XVI, 587.   *Speech on the Middlesex Election, Works*, VII, 59–67.   See also 35 4 and the note on this line, and 17 8, note.

[2] Compare 31 34, note.

[3] Morley's *Burke*, 45.

[4] *Correspondence*, I, 265–269, 272–275.

[5] See 19 24, note ; 17 8, note ; *Works*, I, 496.

of the government are held in trust for the people,[1] and, there-fore, popular impatience must be indulged.   True to his con-servative instincts, he rejected the commonly proposed reforms, —universal suffrage, the disfranchisement of "rotten boroughs," representation for the new trading towns, triennial Parliaments, and the exclusion from the House of men holding offices under the crown.   These plans he regarded as too radical.   "Our Constitution," he urged, "stands on a nice equipoise, with steep precipices and deep waters upon all sides of it.   In removing it from a dangerous leaning towards one side, there may be a risk of oversetting it on the other."[2]   He therefore contented himself with suggesting that the people be stimulated to scru-tinize more closely the conduct of their representatives, and that lists of votes in Parliament be published.   But above all he emphasized the truth upon which he dwells so often in the *Speech on Conciliation,* — the necessity of adapting the govern-ment to the circumstances and temper of the people.[3]   A gov-ernment not so adapted he held to be merely "a scheme upon paper, and not a living, active, effective constitution."[4]

During the years immediately following 1770, Burke devoted his energies to keeping the Rockingham Whigs united against the efforts of the king to win them over.   Without Burke, says Morley, "the Rockingham connection would undoubtedly have fallen to ruin, and with it the most upright, consistent and dis-interested body of men then in public life."[5]   For the sake of this party Burke refused a flattering offer to go to India as one of three commissioners to overhaul the affairs of the East India Company;[6] for the sake of this party he drummed up his

---

[1] See 4 8 and the note on this line.
[2] *Works,* I, 520.   Compare also 51 27, note.
[3] See 9 31 and the note; 19 8 and the note.
[4] *Works,* I, 470.
[5] *Burke,* 62.
[6] *Correspondence,* I, 339.

associates by letter and personal appeal. In carrying out this task he reproached the Duke of Richmond for being "somewhat languid . . . and unsystematic";[1] and the latter made the admission: "Indeed, Burke, you have more credit than any man in keeping us together."[2] Even in this employment as a political whip Burke did not advance the usual cheap arguments for temporary partisan success, but, with that conservatism which deepened with his advancing years, he dwelt rather on the considerations of permanent policy. "Persons in your station of life," he wrote to the Duke of Richmond, "ought to have long views. You people of great families and hereditary trusts and fortunes, . . . if you are what you ought to be, are in my eye the great oaks that shade a country, and perpetuate your benefits from generation to generation. The immediate power of a Duke of Richmond or a Marquis of Rockingham is not so much of moment; but, if their conduct and example hand down their principles to their successors, then their houses become the public repositories and offices of record for the Constitution; not like the tower or Rolls-chapel, where it is searched for and sometimes in vain, in rotten parchments under dripping and perishing walls, but in full vigor, and acting with vital energy and power, in the character of the leading men and natural interests of the country."[3]

From this political activity Burke withdrew for a little while in 1773 for a trip to France. There he saw those royal splendors against which the populace had even then begun to mutter, and he observed in the brilliant society into which he was cordially received two things which he strongly dreaded, atheism and an eager questioning of the "allowed opinions which contribute so much to the public tranquillity."[4] This atheism and this speculation, he perceived, — and he was one of the few who were so clear-sighted, — were working toward

---

[1] *Correspondence,* I, 375.
[2] *Ibid.,* 371.
[3] *Ibid.,* 381, 382.
[4] See 28 2.

revolution. His fear of these tendencies he passionately expressed in Parliament[1] not long after his return. When a bill was pending to abolish the penalties inflicted on religious teachers and schoolmasters who dissented from the doctrines of the Church of England, Burke favored such toleration on the ground that the men from whom the country stood in danger were not the dissenters, but the atheists. " These," he cried, " are the people against whom you ought to aim the shaft of the law ; these are the men to whom, arrayed in all the terrors of government I would say, 'You shall not degrade us into brutes !' . . . The infidels are outlaws of the constitution, not of this country, but of the human race. They are never, never to be supported, never to be tolerated. Under the systematic attacks of these people, I see some of the props of good government already begin to fail."[2]

By this time Burke had won a substantial reputation throughout the United Kingdom. Indeed, as early as the autumn of 1766 several Irish municipalities had voted him the freedom of the city, whereupon his gratified mother had written, " I assure you that it's no honor that is done him that makes me vain of him, but the goodness of his heart, which I believe no man living has a better."[3] During the succeeding years a number of English mercantile organizations also passed resolutions commending his labors in behalf of commerce.[4] Finally, in 1774, when the troubles with America were thickening, Bristol, the trading centre of the west of England, the city which had everything to lose and nothing to gain from a war with the colonies, honored him by electing him as its representative in Parliament.

This election from Bristol furnished Burke with an opportunity to prove that in character as well as in abilities he was removed from the ordinary politician by a whole world of dif-

---

[1] Mar. 17, 1773.
[2] *Speech on the Relief of the Protestant Dissenters, Works,* VII, 35–37.
[3] *Correspondence,* I, 112.   [4] *Ibid.,* 455, 456.

ference. At the conclusion of the poll his colleague had
promised obedience to the instructions of his constituents.
Burke, however, with unexampled boldness, declared his independence : " His [the representative's] unbiased opinion, his
mature judgment, his enlightened conscience, he ought not to
sacrifice to you, to any man or to any set of men living. . . .
Your representative owes you, not his industry only, but his
judgment; and he betrays you instead of serving you, if he
sacrifices it to your opinion. . . . Government and legislation
are matters of reason and judgment, and not of inclination ;
and what sort of reason is that in which the determination
precedes the discussion, in which one set of men deliberate and
another decide, and where those who form the conclusion are
perhaps three hundred miles distant from those who hear the
arguments ? " [1] These principles he heartily followed in practice.
For example, in 1778 a bill was proposed for relaxing some of
the restrictions upon Irish commerce. At once the English
merchants, those of Bristol among the rest, with short-sighted
jealousy raised a cry of protest. But Burke was unmoved. He
boldly spoke and voted for the right side ; and when his constituents besought him to advocate their ideas, he gave such
an answer as few representatives in England or any other
country have ever dared to give : " Is Ireland united to the
crown of Great Britain for no other purpose than that we should
counteract the bounty of Providence in her favor ? . . . Indeed,
Sir, England and Ireland may flourish together. The world is
large enough for us both. Let it be our care not to make ourselves too little for it.[2] . . . You obligingly lament that you are
not to have me for your advocate ; but if I had been capable of
acting as an advocate in opposition to a plan so perfectly consonant to my known principles and to the opinions I had publicly declared on an hundred occasions, I should only disgrace

---

[1] *Speech at the Conclusion of the Poll, Works,* II, 95, 96.
[2] *Two Letters to Gentlemen in Bristol, Works,* II, 252, 253.

myself without supporting with the smallest degree of credit or effect the cause you wished me to undertake. I should have lost the only thing which can make such abilities as mine of any use to the world now or hereafter: I mean that authority which is derived from an opinion that a member speaks the language of truth and sincerity, and that he is not ready to take up or lay down a great political system for the convenience of an hour, that he is in Parliament to support his opinion of the public good, and does not form his opinion in order to get into Parliament, or to continue in it." [1]   These eloquent words fell on deaf ears. Burke was never forgiven for his liberality, and in the election of 1780 he was forced to seek a new constituency.

It was during his six years as member for Bristol that, in the contest over America, Burke rose to his full height as a statesman. Through all the confusion and tangle of the government's temporary shifts and expedients, he steadily urged the necessity of a consistent policy based on the character of the Americans and the permanent relations which should exist between England and her colonies.[2] He was almost alone among the speech-makers of that decade of debate in always going below the superficial considerations of the moment, — a desire for more revenue, irritation at the obstinacy of the colonists, greed of power, — to the fundamental fact that in the long run restraint and violence defeat themselves. Though most members of Parliament seemed incurably ignorant of America and incapable of understanding her point of view, Burke was always well-informed and sympathetic. Indeed, his sympathy, which had led the province of New York to employ him as its London agent,[3] drew upon him many attacks. " I

---

[1] *Two Letters to Gentlemen in Bristol, Works*, II, 257.

[2] See 4 18, note.

[3] This incident is fully discussed by Calvin Stebbins in a paper read before the American Antiquarian Society, Oct. 21, 1893, and published in the *Proceedings* of that body.

am charged with being an American," he wrote to the sheriffs of Bristol. "If warm affection toward those over whom I claim any share of authority be a crime, I am guilty of this charge." [1] Certainly he could plead guilty of doing more than any other Englishman to enlighten his countrymen about America. In addition to many minor speeches scattered through the *Parliamentary History*, he made three great contributions to the subject: the *Speech on American Taxation*, April 19, 1774; the *Speech on Conciliation*, March 22, 1775; and the *Letter to the Sheriffs of Bristol*, April 3, 1777. In the first he argued that the Tea Duty was of no use to England for revenue; that it only served to irritate the Americans; and that by winning the loyalty of the colonists England could get more than she could ever take by force. In the second speech Burke maintained that affairs had come to such a pass that England must conciliate, and that the only way was by yielding. In the *Letter* he reviewed the struggle, and in the light of results justified his own position. Of the three pieces that on *Conciliation* is the best. Not even when dealing with India does Burke excel this in grasp of details, in lucid presentation of a large mass of facts and opinions, and in ripened political wisdom. He virtually summed up everything said on America since he had entered Parliament; he refuted every opposing argument worth serious consideration; and he put every favorable argument in its most convincing form. Then, too, he saw what so many failed to see, that the real cause of the contest lay deeper than the casual orders of a governor or the retaliation of a mob, and that America, in resisting the encroachments of royal prerogative, was fighting a battle for the liberties of Englishmen at home. Thus, with the utmost breadth of view, with an elevation of style which he never surpassed, and with a temperance of expression which he perhaps never again attained, he enunciated principles which are as true for America to-day as

[1] *Works*, II, 222.

they were for England in 1775 : that since laws do not work
in a vacuum, they should not be based upon abstract theory,
but upon experience and policy ;[1] that the first duty of a statesman is, therefore, to study the character and circumstances of
the people whom he governs ;[2] that it is impossible to treat a
nation as a criminal, — *I do not know the method of drawing up
an indictment against a whole people,*[3] — and that the surest conquests are those of peace.

Though Burke could not win over Parliament to his views
on America, yet in 1780 he had better fortune in securing
economies in government expenditure.   He saw the people
staggering under the debt from the American war, and agitating
for a general reform of Parliament and curtailment of the royal
prerogative.   Such changes, however, he regarded as too
radical.   The fault, he argued, was not with the constituencies,
but with the representatives, whom the king had bribed with
sinecure offices.   He proposed, therefore, to abolish some
offices, to consolidate others, and to readjust salaries.   In this
plan he gave further evidence of his grasp of details, for he
comprehended in his scheme of reorganization the vast machine
of the whole civil service and a part of the military.   Burke's
triumph in this undertaking was the more striking, because so
many members of Parliament were directly or indirectly interested in retaining the old abuses.   Doubtless he would never
have succeeded had he not in every step been consistently
conservative, reluctant to touch so much as the semblance of
a vested right.   "I would never suffer any man, . . . " he said,
" to suffer from errors that naturally have grown out of the
abusive constitution of those offices which I propose to regulate.
If I cannot reform with equity, I will not reform at all."[4]

[1] See 37 23–37, and 7 14 and the note on that line.
[2] See 9 27–34.
[3] See 33 22, 23.
[4] *Speech on the Plan for Economical Reform, Works,* II, 322.

One of the offices which Burke had reformed, that of Pay-master of the Forces, he himself occupied in 1782. At that time the North ministry yielded to the Whigs, who were temporarily united under Lord Rockingham, Charles James Fox and Lord Shelburne. Burke, to whom, as we have seen, the party was so deeply indebted, did not get a cabinet place, but only the third-rate position mentioned above. At this exclusion he seems to have been bitterly mortified, for thirteen years later he wrote : "There were few indeed that did not at that time acknowledge . . . that no man in the kingdom better deserved an honorable provision should be made for him."[1] But in spite of his deserts he never received any official post except this, which he held for only a little while. This neglect was due to several causes : he came of an obscure family ; he was needy and improvident ; he was suspected of complicity in the dubious transactions of Richard and of William Burke ; he had many enemies in public life; he was too proud to push his claims ; and, as he grew old, he so far lost control of his temper that he became a troublesome colleague. For these reasons the leading statesman of the day was compelled to stand aside while his inferiors snatched the prizes won by his toil.

The Whigs were scarcely in their seats, when Lord Rocking-ham died and Lord Shelburne became head of the administration. At once Fox and Burke refused to work with him, and by joining their old enemy, Lord North, in what is known as the Coalition, they broke up the Whig party. In this proceeding Burke is accused of deserting his principles for purely personal motives. Certainly his behavior is hard to defend, for he attacked Shelburne with unparalleled asperity ; and, when the Coalition overthrew Shelburne, Burke resumed for a few months the office of Paymaster.

However much his motives or his discretion in regard to most measures of the Coalition may be questioned, yet surely he

[1] *Letter to a Noble Lord, Works,* V, 184.

merits the highest praise for his strenuous advocacy of reform
in the government of India. That unhappy country was then
in the hands of the East India Company, whose system was
corrupt and cruel beyond description, — as Burke puts the
case, unequalled by " all the acts and monuments of peculation, the consolidated corruption of ages, the patterns of
exemplary plunder in the heroic times of Roman iniquity." [1]
Burke knew what he was talking about, knew better than
any man in England, for he had been a member of select committees upon Indian affairs, and he had drawn two of the most
important reports. He is also supposed to have framed the
East India bill commonly known as Fox's. At any rate he
defended it [2] in a speech which, as a whole, ranks but little
below his best, and which, in spite of some extravagance and
some outbursts of temper, perhaps pardonable, contains several
passages in his finest style. It is interesting to compare this
plea for India with his plea for America. In both he displays
the same conservatism, the same distrust of mere theories, and
the same intense hatred of all schemes of government which
rest upon brute force and rob the people of their happiness
and freedom. In beginning his discussion of India he said :
" I feel an insuperable reluctance to giving my hand to destroy
any established institution of government, upon a theory, however plausible it may be." [3] He then proved that his charges
against the East India Company were in no sense theoretical.
With brilliant description and an overwhelming abundance of
evidence he set forth the results of a tyranny which, as he
said, disgraced England and destroyed a large part of the
human species.[4] He could not, however, contend against the
potent influence of the plunder wrung from India ; and thus,
notwithstanding his passionate appeals, the bill was defeated,
and the Coalition, which supported it, was driven from office.

---

[1] *Speech on the Nabob of Arcot's Debts, Works*, III, 49.
[2] Dec. 1, 1783. [3] *Works*, II, 442. [4] *Ibid.*, 536.

The loss of the bill is not to be regretted; for in many respects the measure was unwise, and the reforms at which it aimed Burke finally secured in another way. Early in 1785 he renewed his attack in the *Speech on the Nabob of Arcot's Debts.* Dealing with many complicated financial accounts, with systems of taxation, and with a mass of minute technicalities, — topics which are usually the dryest of the dry, — Burke nevertheless rose almost to the height attained in his *Conciliation with America.* His description of the ravages of Hyder Ali perhaps surpasses anything of the kind in English oratory, but the total effect of the speech is somewhat marred by vituperation. This speech was but preliminary to the famous proceedings against Warren Hastings. When the latter returned to England laden with the spoils of India, Burke felt that the time had come for a telling blow. Accordingly he drew up articles charging Hastings with high crimes and misdemeanors, and in 1786 had the case presented to the House. The story of the trial need not be repeated here, for it has been told by Macaulay in a passage familiar to every one.[1] On this occasion Burke fairly outdid himself as an orator. As he described some of the scenes of havoc in India, every listener, even the prisoner, it is said, was breathless with horror. The trial dragged on till 1795; and, though the verdict at last was for acquittal, Burke had none the less succeeded in reforming the government of India, for he had trumpeted the wrongs of that "emptied and emboweled"[2] land until public sentiment would no longer tolerate them. He was justified in writing, near the close of his life: "If I were to call for a reward, . . . it should be for [the services] in which for fourteen years without intermission I showed the most industry and had the least success: I mean the affairs of India. They are those on which I value myself the most: most for the importance, most for the labor,

---

[1] *Essay on Warren Hastings.*

[2] *Speech on the Nabob of Arcot's Debts, Works,* III, 65.

most for the judgment, most for the constancy and perseverance in the pursuit."[1]

Before the trial of Hastings had closed, the French Revolution had broken out. Burke, who looked upon this, not as the emancipation of oppressed masses, but as an effort of atheists[1] and political theorists[8] to uproot the settled order of society and all hereditary rights in church and state, was horrified. Since his views were hostile to those of the more radical of the Whigs, who on general principles were delighted with a popular uprising, he soon began to draw apart from the men with whom he had been allied against the encroachments of the crown in England and in America. In 1790 he widened the breach still further by an aggressive proclamation of his opinions in *Reflections on the Revolution in France*, his first publication on the subject. The book had, for that day, an enormous sale, and created a profound sensation throughout England, and indeed all Europe. It divided Great Britain into two parties: one composed of Burke and an uncongenial company of Tories and supporters of royal despotism; the other composed of Liberals, many of whom had been Burke's life-long associates. On both sides the feeling ran high; and Burke, already irritated by the disapproval of men whom he held in esteem, was not in a frame of mind to endure assaults calmly. When he was jeered in the House by his former friends, lampooned in the newspapers, and branded as a renegade and traitor, he violently quarreled with Fox, with whom he had been intimate for years, replied to taunts with pamphlets of increasing acrimony, but never flinched from his course. Notwithstanding the censure heaped upon him, his attitude is not surprising to any one who carefully studies his writings and speeches in their chronological order, for he had been steadily growing more conservative. The

[1] *Letter to a Noble Lord, Works*, V, 192.
[2] *Reflections on the Revolution in France, Works*, III, 378.
[8] *Ibid.*, 399, 418.

seeming contradiction between his early adherence to the cause of
the people and his later adherence to the cause of the sovereign
was due in part to this natural change and in part to his desire
to preserve the balance between king and subject : in England
the crown had been the transgressor ; in France, he thought, the
people.[1]   Moreover, he had always insisted that liberty is " inseparable from order "; [2] and in the French Revolution he saw
nothing but disorder.[3]   He had always insisted that no institution should be overturned unless corrupt beyond reform ; [4] and
he believed that the institutions of France could be reformed.[5]

In the *Reflections*, in spite of bitterness against the National
Assembly and the Englishmen who commended it, Burke dis-
played much real wisdom.   He saw from the beginning the
advancing shadow of the Reign of Terror ; [6] he predicted the
rise of a military dictator,[7] and he pointed out the fatal defect
of the several theoretical devices of the constitution of France,
such as the geometrical division of representative districts.[8]
But the *Reflections* contains almost the last of his sober thinking on the matter ; for, as the Revolution progressed, he became
more and more wrought up, so that in each of his succeeding
utterances, —*Letter to a Member of the National Assembly*,
Appeal from the New to the Old Whigs, *Thoughts on French
Affairs*, *Remarks on the Policy of the Allies*, *Observations on the
Conduct of the Minority* and *Letters on a Regicide Peace*, — the
reasoning grew feebler, the scolding shriller.   At last he was
nearly frantic with rage at the slaughters during the Reign of
Terror, and frantic with fear of a revolution in England.   So

---

[1] *Appeal from the New to the Old Whigs, Works*, IV, 92–94.

[2] *Letter to a Noble Lord, Works*, V, 183.

[3] *Appeal from the New to the Old Whigs, Works*, IV, 97.

[4] Pages xxxii, xxxiv ; *Appeal from the New to the Old Whigs, Works*,
IV, 80 ; *Reflections on the Revolution in France, Works*, III, 562.

[5] *Letter to a Member of the National Assembly, Works*, IV, 42–52.

[6] *Works*, III, 339.   [8] *Ibid.*, 461–476.

[7] *Ibid.*, 524, 525.

irrational is public excitement, however, that, while his opinions were losing real value, his influence was strengthening. As the events which he had predicted came to pass one by one, the laughter of his enemies turned to alarm ; and finally, when Louis the Sixteenth was executed in 1793, England, though in no serious danger, was filled with consternation and looked to Burke as her most far-sighted statesman. Yet to his credit be it said that, even with the nation applauding his frenzy, he now and then fell back into his early habit of examining a question in all lights. In such a moment of clear vision, when he perceived that the movement in France might be one of actual progress, when he caught a glimpse of himself as posterity views him, he penned the solemn close of his *Thoughts on French Affairs* : " I have done with this subject, I believe, forever. It has given me many anxious moments for the two last years. If a great change is to be made in human affairs, the minds of men will be fitted to it, the general opinions and feelings will draw that way. Every fear, every hope, will forward it; and then they who persist in opposing this mighty current in human affairs will appear rather to resist the decrees of Providence itself than the mere designs of men. They will not be resolute and firm, but perverse and obstinate." [1]

Burke's mistakes in regard to the French Revolution are by some critics ascribed in part to his imperfect acquaintance with the subject.[2] However that may be, it is certain that during the same period, when he was dealing with a subject on which he was thoroughly informed, Ireland, he showed his old qualities of statesmanship. He had always been a champion of his down-trodden native land, just as he had been a champion of America and India. In his boyhood, as we have seen, he endeavored to master the history of his " poor country"; and later he tried to secure justice for it, though at the

[1] *Works*, IV, 377.
[2] Morley's *Burke*, 160.

expense of offending his Bristol constituents. Then, when Ireland caught the contagion of the French Revolution, and when the war between England and France rendered the situation still more threatening, Burke urged for Ireland the same policy which he had urged for America seventeen years before, —conciliation. In letter and pamphlet he unceasingly advocated relieving the Catholics of their disabilities. "It passes my comprehension," he wrote, "in what manner it is that men can be reconciled to the *practical* merits of a constitution . . . by being *practically* excluded from any of its advantages." [1] This is surely a return to the high level of the dictum, "I do not know the method of drawing up an indictment against a whole people."

The incidents connected with the close of the trial of Warren Hastings, with the excitement over the French Revolution, and with the agitation for toleration in Ireland mark the end of Burke's public career. In 1794, with his fame restored, he retired from Parliament. He was to have received a peerage with the title Lord Beaconsfield; but, since the death of his son left him without a direct heir to whom to transmit the honor, he accepted instead a pension granted in recognition of his services to the country. This pension was the occasion of a fresh attack upon him by his enemies. He replied in the *Letter to a Noble Lord*, which from a rhetorical point of view is one of his best pieces of work. He survived but three years, during which he wrote the *Letters on a Regicide Peace*. He died on the ninth of July, 1797.

The personality of Burke, which in his public life seems a little vague and distant, appears with more distinctness in his private life. As described by Madame D'Arblay he was tall, his figure noble, his air commanding, his address graceful, his voice clear, penetrating, sonorous and powerful, his language

---

[1] *Second Letter to Sir Hercules Langrishe on the Catholic Question, Works.* VI, 382.

copious, various and eloquent, his manners attractive, his conversation delightful. " Since we lost Garrick," she wrote, " I
have seen nobody so enchanting." [1] The range of Burke's
conversation was an indication of the variety of his interests,
— politics, economics, social problems, history, philosophy,
poetry, drama, painting, sculpture, science, agriculture, manufactures. Whatever subject he took up, he pursued with the
same *furor* that possessed him in studying at college and in
mastering the details of finance and the affairs of America and
India. When he turned from the cares of state to his farm at
Beaconsfield, he was eager over carrots and pigs, just as he
had been eager over the Stamp Act. [2]

Furthermore, his zeal in behalf of the wretched and the
oppressed was not a mere vague sentiment which expended
itself in words : it was a ruling motive in his daily conduct.
When the poet Crabbe was obscure and penniless, Burke took
him into the family at Beaconsfield, found a printer for his
verses, and finally obtained for him a living in the church.
Burke sent the painter Barry abroad and for five years furnished him with money for study and travel. [3] During the
Revolution he kept open house for the French refugees, gave
from his own slender purse to acquaintances whose estates had
been confiscated, [4] and established near Beaconsfield a school
for French orphans and children of *émigrés* who had suffered
losses. [5] Such open-handed liberality could not but win him
troops of staunch friends. Richard Shackleton was devoted
to him from boyhood to old age ; Sir Joshua Reynolds appointed him an executor and left him a large legacy ; Dr.
Johnson, the stout Tory who declared that "the first Whig was

---

[1] *Diary and Letters*, June, 1782.
[2] *Correspondence*, I, 245–251, 257–265.
[3] *Ibid.*, 86–92, 116–129.
[4] *Ibid.*, IV, 246–251.
[5] *Ibid.*, 331–341.

the devil,"[1] admired and loved him. Burke's faults were clearly those of an ardent temperament, — at times unreasoning zeal for persons, parties or causes, and an impatience of contradiction and delay which betrayed him into fiery outbursts of passion. His virtues were also those of an ardent temperament, — unquenchable energy, exhaustless generosity.

In his family relations he was very happy. In the winter of 1756–1757 he had married Jane Nugent, the daughter of a physician. She was a woman of gentle manners, even temper, and a capacity for management which lifted many burdens from her husband's shoulders. Though Burke's only son, Richard, was not generally liked, he was idolized by his father, who with characteristic eagerness had indulged in the most extravagant hopes of a brilliant future for him. The death of Richard in 1794 was a blow from which Burke never recovered : it filled his last days with gloom, and hastened his end. " I am alone," he wrote. "I have none to meet my enemies in the gate."[2]

V.

Burke as a Statesman.[3]

Burke's principles of statesmanship, when briefly set down, seem almost too bald and simple to be worth much attention. One should remember, however, that theories of government

---

[1] Boswell's *Life of Johnson*, III, 326.

[2] *Letter to a Noble Lord*, *Works*, V, 208.

[3] Able discussions of Burke's statesmanship are to be found in section 9 of chapter xii of Leslie Stephen's *History of English Thought in the Eighteenth Century*, New York, 1876 ; and in John Morley's *Edmund Burke : a Historical Study*, London, 1867. The latter book should not be confounded with Morley's life of Burke in the *English Men of Letters*, to which reference has already been made. Stephen dwells on a matter for which there is no space in this introduction, the sources from which Burke drew his ideas in statesmanship

had not in Burke's day been discussed and developed as they have been since, so that what is trite now may have been novel then: moreover, statesmanship does not consist in a mere knowledge of maxims, — in which a modern schoolboy might equal Burke, — but in understanding when and how to apply them.

The basis of Burke's system is explained in a sentence from one of his letters: "The principles of true politics are those of morality enlarged; and I neither now do, nor ever will, admit of any other."[1] But had he never written this sentence, his works are full of proofs that his aim was the triumph of the good: among the orators of his time he is notable for his frequent appeals to the love of right rather than to the love of might. It is better, he held, to try to make a government wise and honest than to try to make it strong.[2] His hatred of the French Revolutionists was due partly to his conviction that they were enemies to sound morals: they were overturning the church, a bulwark of morality; they were dishonestly repudiating debts; they were unjustly confiscating property. Of their action he wrote: "As no one of us men can dispense with public or private faith, or with any other tie of moral obligation, so neither can any number of us. The number engaged in crimes, instead of turning them into laudable acts, only augments the quantity and intensity of the guilt."[3]

The first of the moral principles on which Burke rested great weight was justice. Where duller men would have been stolidly indifferent, his powerful imagination enabled him to feel keenly the burdens of the oppressed. Thus it was for justice to the clergy and the nobility of France, to the disfranchised Catholics, and to the swarming millions of India, that he made his most fervent pleas. Such pleas were not "splendid

---

[1] Letter to the Bishop of Chester, 1771, *Correspondence*, I, 332.
[2] *Letter to the Sheriffs of Bristol, Works*, II, 220.
[3] *Appeal from the New to the Old Whigs, Works*, IV, 163.

commonplaces " at that time ; for the idea that a nation was
bound by the same code of justice as an individual was far less
generally accepted than now.   Every European power regarded
the acquisition of territory as ample excuse for unprovoked
rapine and slaughter, — as is proved by the very crimes of
Hastings which Burke labored to punish, by the general sympathy for the great criminal, by the defence that he had extended
the bounds of the British Empire, and by his final acquittal.
Such pleas as Burke's are not "splendid commonplaces" to-
day ; for although the civilized world ought long since to have
discovered the "ill-husbandry of injustice,"[1] scarcely a year
passes without some outrage committed against a weaker nation
by a stronger.

A second principle to which Burke often appealed is, — as
might be expected from his character, — generosity.   When
leading statesmen held the belief, still common among ignorant
people, that the surest method of enlarging national commerce
is to restrict and retaliate, Burke advocated liberality.   His
narrow-minded constituents remonstrated, but he replied with
a truth which is not yet well understood: " It is but too natural for us to see our own *certain* ruin in the *possible* prosperity
of other people.   It is hard to persuade us that everything
which is *got* by another is not *taken* from ourselves.   But it is
fit that we should get the better of these suggestions, which
come from what is not the best and soundest part of our
nature."[2]   When Burke's colleagues maintained that they
were dealing justly with America, he answered that they should
not be content with mere grudging justice, but should follow
the higher policy of generosity.   This idea underlies all his
utterances on America, and the special emphasis which he
lays on it in the *Speech on Conciliation* is perhaps the one thing
which makes that the noblest of his productions.   " Magna-

[1] See 45 21.
[2] *Two Letters to Gentlemen in Bristol, Works,* II, 260.

nimity in politics," he said in closing, "is not seldom the truest wisdom ; and a great empire and little minds go ill together. . . . Our ancestors have made the most extensive, and the only honorable conquests, not by destroying but by promoting the wealth, the number, the happiness of the human race."[1] This same ideal, which seems almost as far from realization to-day as it was in 1797, he presented again in almost his last piece of writing : " Not . . . a sort of England detached from the rest of the world, and amusing herself with the puppet-show of a naval power, . . . but . . . that sort of England who, sympathetic with the adversity or the happiness of mankind, felt that nothing in human affairs was foreign to her."[2]

Many men have been as zealous as Burke for justice and generosity, but comparatively few have added to their zeal the saving knowledge that perfect justice can never be attained in this world ; that human institutions are at best "compromises, sometimes between good and evil and sometimes between evil and evil."[3] By this knowledge he was kept from being a stickler for abstract principles, a theorist. He never advocated, except in the case of the French Revolution, mere technical rights, which may be "the most odious of all wrongs and the most vexatious of all injustice."[4] The thing for which he looked was the utilitarian effect, "the happiness of the whole,"[5] or, to use Bentham's phrase, "the greatest happiness of the greatest number." In theory the British Constitution, for example, might be as illogical as possible : if as a matter of fact it protected person and property, Burke was well content to let it stand unchanged. "A man of warm speculative benevolence," he wrote, "may wish his society otherwise con-

---

[1] Pages 73, 74.
[2] *First Letter on a Regicide Peace, Works*, V, 244, 245.
[3] *Reflections on the Revolution in France, Works*, III, 313.
[4] See 35 8–10; 7 14, note.
[5] *Speech on the Petition of the Unitarians, Works*, VII, 45.

stituted than he finds it ; but a good patriot, and a true politician, always considers how he shall make the most of the
existing materials of his country." [1]

Burke's antipathy to mere theories also saved him from the
fallacy of supposing that the machinery of government may
be constructed as if men were uniform, passive units. This
error, which was rife among his predecessors and contemporaries, [2] persists to this day in the minds of those who attempt to
suppress evil or reorganize society on the assumption that the
enactment of a law will make men wise, temperate, industrious,
frugal or unselfish. Burke, however, seized every opportunity
to sneer at such " speculative projects " [3] and " paper government." [4] He invariably tried, as in the *Speech on Conciliation*, [5]
to take into account temper and environment. " I never," he
protested, "was wild enough to conceive that one method
would serve for the whole, that the natives of Hindostan and
those of Virginia could be ordered in the same manner." [6]

These several phases of Burke's bent for the practical rather
than the theoretical point of view are, in the last analysis, a
trust in experience, — a theme on which he was never tired of
dwelling. Men might offer any number of *a priori* arguments :
he simply replied that conjectures were interesting, but not
convincing. " Fortunately I am not obliged to tax my own
unproductive invention. . . . I only wish you to return to that
mode which a uniform experience has marked out to you as
best." [7]

A man who clings so tenaciously to experience is likely to be
an uncompromising conservative ; and Burke was no exception

---

[1] *Reflections on the Revolution in France, Works,* III, 440.

[2] Stephen's *History of English Thought in the Eighteenth Century,*
II, 211.

[3] See 6 15, note.

[4] See 6 15.

[5] See pages 9–25.

[6] *Letter to the Sheriffs of Bristol, Works,* II, 227.

[7] See 49 15–27.

to the rule. Changes, he thought, should always be gradual, and should be made only when imperatively necessary.
Indeed, so strong was his reverence for the wisdom of the
ages that he was willing to tolerate abuses till they actually
struck "at the root of order."[1] Then he was moved to act,
for few things were dearer to his heart than a quiet, well-regu-
lated state. Whatever interfered with this, whether rebellion,
riot, usurpation, radical reforms, agitation, or the questioning
of traditional beliefs in religion or politics, he was prompt to
withstand. Such a man, with his face set toward the past, is
not well fitted to deal with new social and political conditions,
which demand experiments ; and yet without the restraining
influence of such men a whole nation might by a rash leap lose
the fruit of much toil and pain. Each age, then, must have its
conservatives as well as its progressives ; and Burke, with his
passion for good government, whether in England, America,
Ireland, India or France, was for his generation — as indeed
he has been for all generations since — "the great pleader for
conservatism."

VI.

BURKE AS AN ORATOR.[2]

Though it is customary to speak of Burke as a great orator,
the fact is that he frequently produced no immediate effect.
These failures were due to several causes, one of which was
his unprepossessing appearance. However much Miss Burney[3]
may have been charmed when she first met him, yet as he rose
in Parliament he was not attractive with his heavy, Quaker-like

---

[1] *Tract on the Popery Laws, Works,* VI, 340.

[2] Burke's oratory and his style are discussed at some length in Morley's
Burke, in Goodrich's *Select British Eloquence,* and the introductions to
Payne's edition of the *Select Works* and to Professor Bliss Perry's *Selections
from Burke,* Henry Holt Company, New York, 1896.

[3] Afterwards Madame D'Arblay.

figure, scratch wig, round spectacles and a cumbrous roll of paper loading his pocket. [1] To these disadvantages he added clumsy gestures, a voice somewhat harsh when he spoke in public, a strong Irish brogue, and at times a hurried articulation. Moreover in later years he now and then spoiled a speech by losing his temper. But above all, he was deficient in tact : often he either overestimated the capacity of his hearers or else he refused to condescend to it. They wanted a concise presentation of leading points : he insisted upon viewing the matter from every side and in every light. They were too slow-witted to comprehend anything except the obvious : he insisted upon applying profound principles. They were looking for personal or partisan advantage : he offered them maxims of statesmanship. He was, as Goldsmith drew him, a speaker

> Who, too deep for his hearers, still went on refining,
> And thought of convincing while they thought of dining. [2]

Indeed, by some of the younger wits he was called "the dinner-bell." So widely did he miss the mark that the *Speech on the Nabob of Arcot's Debts* did not impress Pitt and Grenville as worth a reply, and the *Speech on Conciliation* emptied the benches.

In spite of these mistakes in casting pearls of philosophy and statesmanship before the House, Burke was at times unsurpassed. His first speeches, as has been said, "filled the town with wonder", and during his earlier career many of his contributions to the debates were so compact, pointed, and telling [3] that he was everywhere recognized as one of the ablest speakers in Parliament. Finally, at the trial of Hastings he swept his audience up to a pitch of uncontrollable emotion. These

---

[1] Green's *History of the English People*, IV, 234.

[2] *Retaliation.*

[3] Few of these speeches have been printed in his collected *Works*, but some of them appear in brief reports in the *Parliamentary History*.

triumphs, which establish beyond peradventure his fame as an orator, were due in part to his natural ardor, which in his happiest moments kindled all who came within range of his voice. He owed yet more of his success to his amazing knowledge of his subjects. He had never visited India, for example : nevertheless he had read and studied huge masses of facts about that country, and had animated them by his imagination until, as Macaulay puts it, " India and its inhabitants were not to him, as to most Englishmen, mere names and abstractions, but a real country and a real people. The burning sun, the strange vegetation of the palm and the cocoa-tree, the ricefield, the tank, the huge trees older than the Mogul Empire, under which the village crowds assemble, the thatched roof of the peasant's hut, the rich tracery of the mosque where the imaum prays with his face to Mecca, the drums and banners and gaudy idols, the devotee swinging in the air, the graceful maiden with the pitcher on her head, descending the steps to the river-side, the black faces, the long beards, the yellow streaks of sect, the turbans and the flowing robes, the spears and the silver maces, the elephants with their canopies of state, the gorgeous palanquin of the prince, and the close litter of the noble lady, — all these things were to him as the objects amidst which his own life had been passed, as the objects which lay on the road between Beaconsfield and St. James's Street." [1] With all India thus present to his eye, Burke drew pictures of such startling reality, he showed such thorough and easy mastery of every detail, that his listeners could not but value his opinion as that of a man who knew everything to be known about the matter ; they could not help feeling with him that " oppression in Bengal was the same thing as oppression in the streets of London." [2]

---

[1] *Essay on Warren Hastings.* Goodrich has already quoted this passage to illustrate the same point.

[2] Macaulay's *Essay on Warren Hastings.* The phrase was evidently suggested by a sentence from Burke's *Speech in Opening the Impeachment*

Other important elements in Burke's oratory are the brilliancy of expression and the logical development of ideas, — elements which have helped to give lasting influence to some of the speeches which at the moment were failures. An instance in point is the *Speech on the Nabob of Arcot's Debts,* which Erskine is said to have slept through, but which he afterwards thumbed to pieces in the printed copy. These qualities, however, may be discussed more properly in relation to Burke's style.

VII.

BURKE AS A WRITER.

One of the first things to strike the reader of Burke is the vigor which he displays in nearly every kind of prose : in never-to-be-forgotten descriptions of the soft beauty of Marie Antoinette or of the horrors of war in India ; in blood-curdling tales of the cruelty of Debi Sing at Rungpore ; in clear-cut expositions of the effect of poetry upon the emotions, or the effect of Popery laws in Ireland ; in arguments for toleration or conciliation which carry one along with the rush of rapid narrative ; in the pathos of his laments for the death of his son ; in the irony of the *Vindication of Natural Society ;* in the terrific invective of the *Letters on a Regicide Peace ;* in the splendor of the appeal at the close of the *Speech on Conciliation ;* in the unadorned gravity of the *Address to the King.* Through all this range, from which humor alone is excluded, Burke moves with a sure and imperious stride.

Since there is no notable piece of description in the *Speech on Conciliation,* the student of Burke's style should read such a

of Warren Hastings, Second Day, *Works,* IX, 448 : " The laws of morality are the same everywhere, and . . . there is no action which would pass for an act of extortion, of peculation, of bribery and of oppression in England, that is not an act of extortion, of peculation, of bribery and oppression in Europe, Asia, Africa and all the world over."

passage as that which tells of the tortures at Rungpore [1] or of the devastation of the Carnatic by Hyder Ali. [2] Two fragments from the latter are worth quoting here to show in what large measure Burke had the poet's power of realizing by the imagination a scene on which his eyes had never rested : " All the horrors of war before known or heard of were mercy to that new havoc. A storm of universal fire blasted every field, consumed every house, destroyed every temple. The miserable inhabitants, flying from their flaming villages, in part were slaughtered ; others, without regard to sex, to age, to the respect of rank or sacredness of function, fathers torn from children, husbands from wives, enveloped in a whirlwind of cavalry, and amidst the goading spears of drivers and the trampling of pursuing horses, were swept into captivity in an unknown and hostile land. Those who were able to evade this tempest fled to the walled cities ; but escaping from fire, sword and exile, they fell into the jaws of famine. . . . For eighteen months without intermission this destruction raged from the gates of Madras to the gates of Tanjore ; and so completely did these masters in their art, Hyder Ali and his more ferocious son, absolve themselves of their impious vow, that, when the British armies traversed, as they did, the Carnatic for hundreds of miles in all directions, through the whole line of their march they did not see one man, not one woman, not one child, not one four-footed beast of any description whatever. One dead, uniform silence reigned over the whole region." [3]

In exposition Burke has done nothing better in small compass than his explanation of the causes of the American love of freedom in this *Speech on Conciliation.* [4] As regards choice

---

[1] *Speech in Opening the Impeachment of Warren Hastings,* Third Day, *Works,* X, 83–90.

[2] This bit is in Professor Perry's *Selections from Burke,* a book which, though it contains nothing from the *Speech on Conciliation,* is useful for the study of Burke's style in general.

[3] *Works,* III, 63–65.   [4] Pages 19–25.

of words as well as arrangement of ideas the English language hardly furnishes a better model of expository method. Here, as in Burke's descriptions and narrations, definite words bite the meaning into the mind, and concrete examples vivify the general statements. The effect of such specific terms is well brought out by Payne,[1] who compares a quotation from this passage with one from Lord Brougham which is made up of general, or abstract, words :

In large bodies the circulation of power must be less vigorous at the extremities. Nature has said it. The Turk cannot govern Egypt and Arabia and Kurdistan as he governs Thrace ; nor has he the same dominion in Crimea and Algiers which he has at Brusa and Smyrna. Despotism itself is obliged to truck and huckster. The Sultan gets such obedience as he can. — Pages 24, 25.

In all the despotisms of the East it has been observed that the further any part of the empire is removed from the capital the more do its inhabitants enjoy some sort of rights and privileges ; the more inefficacious is the power of the monarch ; and the more feeble and easily decayed is the organization of the government. — *Inquiry into the Colonial Policy of the European Powers.*

These two bits show clearly enough Burke's superiority and one of the sources of it.

Another excellent example — this time argumentative — is the paragraph beginning " Ireland before the English conquest."[2] Here figurative touches are not infrequent, but the figures are simple, even colloquial : " The *roots* of our primitive constitution were early *transplanted into that soil*, and *grew* and *flourished* there " ;[3] " Your ancestors did not churlishly *sit down* alone to the *feast* of Magna Charta " ;[4] " *Your standard could never be advanced an inch* before your privileges."[5] The whole speech, in fact, is strewn with such turns, which perhaps do more than anything else to impart vitality to a style : " The

[1] Burke's *Select Works*, I, xxxix.   [4] 42 31, 32.
[2] 42 17.   [3] 42 26–28.   [5] 43 2, 3.

public would not have patience to see us *play the game out*" ;[1]
" They are not *squeezed into this happy form* by the constraints
of watchful and suspicious government " ;[2] " They will *cling* and
grapple to you " ;[3] " I *put my foot in the tracks* of our forefathers,
where I can neither *wander* nor *stumble.*"[4]

But Burke's exuberant imagination would not allow him to
stop at such simple tropes. His mind was teeming with suggestions of subtle likenesses and relations, — suggestions which,
when translated into words, became similes or metaphors, many
of which surpass in poetic force most of the verse of his century. Oddly enough, as Macaulay notes, his imagination grew
more active, his style more florid, with his advancing years. In
his youth, in the *Inquiry into the Origin of our Ideas on the
Sublime and Beautiful,* " he wrote on the emotions produced by
mountains and cascades, by the masterpieces of painting and
sculpture, by the faces and necks of beautiful women, in the
style of a parliamentary report. In his old age he discussed
treaties and tariffs in the most fervid and brilliant language of
romance."[5] It is interesting to notice the gradual change.
The *Inquiry* contains only one or two bits which can be called
flowery, such as " In the morning of our days, when the senses
are unworn and tender."[6] There is one bold metaphor, " In
this description the terrible and sublime *blaze out* together."[7]
At the period of the *Speech on Conciliation* Burke was at his
best, splendid and yet restrained. The page[8] containing the
sentence, " If . . . that angel should have drawn up the curtain and unfolded the rising glories of his country," and the
impassioned peroration with the imagery of " the sanctuary of
liberty, the sacred temple consecrated to our common faith,"[9]
— these passages, though in a manner to be attempted by a
genius only, and even then too ornate for modern taste, were

[1] 5 24, 25.   [4] 51 27, 28.   [7] *Ibid.,* 140.
[2] 17 13, 14.   [5] *Essay on Lord Bacon.*   [8] 14.
[3] 72 2.   [6] *Works,* I, 97.   [9] 72 10, 11.

for the time and place proper and effective. But ten years later in the *Speech on the Nabob of Arcot's Debts* Burke passed the bounds set by an age when the florid was more admired than now, the repulsive more readily tolerated. Of all the "purple patches," however, the most gorgeous is in the *Reflections on the Revolution*, the description of Marie Antoinette, which begins, " Surely never lighted on this orb, which she hardly seemed to touch, a more delightful vision. I saw her just above the horizon, decorating and cheering the elevated sphere she just began to move in,—glittering like the morning star, full of life and splendor and joy." [1]

Such opulence of style was in no sense an affectation. But though it was his natural mode of expression, he has left two noteworthy exceptions, the austerely phrased *Report on the Lords' Journal*, 1794, and the sober *Address to the King*, 1777. The latter contains a passage deemed by some the noblest Burke ever wrote. It begins, "What, gracious sovereign, is the empire of America to us, or the empire of the world, if we lose our own liberties ? " [2]

This sentence, which is modeled upon the well-known verse from St. Matthew, "What is a man profited if he shall gain the whole world and lose his own soul ? " [3] is one of many in which Burke, though an independent writer, has enriched his style either by direct quotation or by adaptation from the Bible. In this very *Speech on Conciliation* there are upwards of twenty of these passages, [4] such as, " *When the day-star* of the English Constitution *had arisen in their hearts.*" [5] In like manner Burke drew upon the Roman and the English poets, especially Virgil, Horace and Juvenal, Shakspere, Milton

---

[1] *Works*, III, 331.   [2] *Ibid.*, VI, 177.   [3] xvi, 26.

[4] The parallels are pointed out in the notes to the following lines : 4 16, 13 32, 14 31, 24 29, 30 4, 30 6, 31 16, 31 27, 37 1, 38 5, 46 6, 49 8, 50 33, 51 22, 51 30, 51 31, 63 16, 72 12, 72 20, 73 25, 73 34.

[5] 46 6, 7.

and Pope.[1]   Indeed it is said that whenever he wrote, he kept a "ragged Delphin Virgil" near his elbow. He was thoroughly acquainted, not only with the writers just mentioned, but with others of the best, including Plutarch, Plautus, Terence, Cicero, Lucretius, Bacon and Dryden.   In spite of his knowledge of literature and in spite of the current fashion of quoting, particularly from the Greek and Latin classics, Burke seldom erred by quoting too frequently or by patching an incongruous element into the context.   Having reached the right pitch of thought or expression, then, by the poetic force of a borrowed turn, by the familiarity and power of suggestion or by the aptness, he added the finishing touch.

Brilliant as Burke's phrasing is, he did not rely upon mere brilliancy : he was generally careful to arrange his thoughts so that each fell into its proper place and contributed its due share towards the total effect.   His skill in planning need not be discussed here, for at a glance it is evident in the analysis of the *Speech on Conciliation* a few pages farther on.

Moreover, Burke took every precaution to make the logical relations of his ideas unmistakable.   For this purpose he used many connective words or phrases.   For example, the first line of each paragraph on pages 35 and 36 contains a phrase which serves as a connective with what precedes : "There is, Sir, *also* a circumstance which convinces me that *this mode of criminal proceeding*";[2]   "*In this situation*, let us seriously and coolly ponder";[3]   "If *then the removal of the causes of this spirit of American liberty*";[4]   "If we adopt *this mode.*"[5] Another of Burke's methods was to construct the paragraph so as to throw as much emphasis as possible upon the main idea in it.   By a word or phrase at the beginning he would indicate

---

[1] See 14 10, 17 4, 18 6, 19 31, 22 31, 24 8, 24 25, 25 18, 26 2, 30 4, 31 9, 32 33, 37 19, 46 9, 49 2, 49 21, 51 16, 51 20, 63 2, 69 27, 70 29, 70 33, 71 34, 72 2, 73 1, 73 17.

[2] 35 19, 20.   [3] 36 1.   [4] 36 12, 13.   [5] 36 19.

the topic; he would next present the various details; and he would close with a summarizing phrase or sentence. A good instance is the paragraph beginning " The proposition is peace." [1] This sentence names the topic, *peace.* Then come several explanations, and at the end the gist of the whole matter, " To reconcile them to each other in the same act and by the bond of the same interest which reconciles them to the British government." The next two paragraphs are constructed in much the same way. The artifices just mentioned are but two out of many, for Burke was expert in most of the devices used in writing good prose.

Every criticism of Burke's style, however, is wholly inadequate. To say that he is vigorous, brilliantly imaginative, at times severely simple, at times florid, to say that he quotes aptly, arranges his ideas logically and is dexterous in constructing sentences and paragraphs, — all this is much like saying that a human being is made up of water, iron, lime, carbon and sodium. The most important element still eludes the analysis of the chemist and the critic. The only way, then, to understand Burke and his style is to study him and see for oneself how " a generous nature took her own way to perfection."

VIII.

STRUCTURE OF THE SPEECH ON CONCILIATION.

The *Speech on Conciliation* is one of the best examples of Burke's skill in organizing material so that each idea falls into its proper place and contributes its due share to the total effect. This perfection of structure is most easily seen in a skeleton, or outline, in which the divisions stand out clearly. Such an outline may be drawn in several forms, but the one here chosen is the argumentative brief, which is treated minutely in the third chapter of Professor G. P. Baker's *Principles of Argumentation*.[1] According to this scheme the main body of the argument is included in the *brief proper*. In this part the lettering and numbering of heads does not indicate the relative importance of arguments, but merely their relation to the chief proposition. Thus arguments marked with capital Roman numerals directly support the proposition ; those marked with capital letters support the arguments marked with capital Roman numerals, and so on. The arguments in support of a statement are always arranged under it — the reverse of the order of the syllogism. In cases where Burke has presented his material in the form of the syllogism, arguments first and then conclusion, his order has been changed for a few sentences. The numbers in parentheses in the following partial brief refer to pages and lines of the text. It is suggested that the pupil substitute a sentence for each dash, but that he be given a good deal of help in the case of references without dashes.

INTRODUCTION.

I. The return of the "grand penal bill" gives a fresh opportunity to choose a plan for dealing with America. (3 1–25)

II. The subject is a most serious one. (4 1)

    A. Since it was the most important matter before Parliament when Burke took his seat, he was at more than common pains to instruct himself in regard to it. (4 2–19)

    B. ——— (4 20–27)

    C. ——— (4 28–31)

    D. ——— (4 32–5 8)

III. It is evident that those who are opposing the action of the government must present a definite policy. (5 9–32)

    A. ——— (5 33–6 13)

    B. ——— (6 14–25)

    C. ——— (6 26–7 9)

---

[1] Boston, 1895. See also revised edition by Baker and Huntington, 1905.

IV. Burke's proposition is to secure peace by removing the grounds of difference. (7 10–25)

V. This simple plan, though it has none of the splendor of Lord North's project, and does not propose an auction of finance, derives advantage from the proposition and registry of Lord North's project (7 26–8 15); for

    A. —— (8 16–20)
    B. —— (8 21–32)
    C. —— (8 33–9 4)

VI. The proposal for peace ought to come from England (9 8, 9); for

    A. —— (9 6, 7)
    B. —— (9 10–18)

VII. There are two leading questions to consider: (9 19)

    A. —— (9 20)
    B. —— (9 21)

VIII. The determination of both these questions depends, not upon abstract ideas and general theories, but upon the nature and circumstances of America. (9 22–10 4)

BRIEF PROPER.

England should secure peace by conciliation, because

  I. The condition of America requires this method; for

    A. —— (10 5–11 7)
    B. —— (11 8–12); for
    (11 13–15 19)
    C. —— (16 1–13)
    D. —— (16 14–17 21)

Refutation.

  II. The argument that we should use force because America is worth fighting for is untenable (17 22–18 3); for

    A. Force is temporary. (18 4–7)
    B. It is uncertain. (18 8–14)
    C. It impairs the object. (18 15–27)
    D. We have no experience in favor of force. (18 28–34)

Direct Proof.

III. The temper and character of the Americans make it necessary for us to conciliate them (19 1–9); for

    A. The spirit of liberty is stronger among them than among any other people on earth (19 10–25 12)

IV. Coercion —— (25 24–26 23); for

    (26 24–28 12)

 V. Of the three possible methods of dealing with America, ——, ——, and ——, the last is the only one possible (28 13–30); for

    A. —— (28 31–29 2); for

        I. —— (29 3–31 9)

        2. —— (31 10–11); for

            (31 12–33 3)

    B. —— (33 4–11); for

    (33 12–36 11)

    C. —— (36 12–18); for

        I. —— (36 19–31)

Refutation.

        2. —— (36 32–37 25); for

            (37 26–38 18)

        3. —— (39 1–20); for

            (40 3–41 11)

        4. —— (41 12–19); for

            (41 20–27)

Direct Proof.

        5. —— (41 28–42 13); for

            (42 14–48 3)

        6. —— (48 4–7); for

            (48 8–31)

        7. —— (48 32–49 14); for

          a. —— (49 15–52 2); for

[Here are inserted from time to time the resolutions which express in formal terms the ideas already presented.]

Refutation.

         i. —— (52 3–53 4)

         ii. —— (53 20–54 7)

Direct Proof.

iii. —— (54 8–14); for

    y. —— (54 15–56 2)

Refutation.

    z. —— (56 3–12); for

    (56 13–28)

Direct Proof.

iv. —— (56 29–57 28)

b. —— (57 29–58 27); for

    (58 28–59 34)

c. —— (60 1–15); for

    (60 16–33)

Refutation.

d. —— (61 9–17); for

    (61 18–63 34)

e. —— (64 1–9); for

    (64 10–22)

f. —— (64 23–34); for

    (65 1–68 27)

g. —— (69 17, 18); for

    (69 19–71 6)

h. —— (71 7–28)

Direct Proof.

8. —— (71 29–72 19); for

    (72 20–74 10)

CHRONOLOGICAL TABLE.

Life of Burke.	General History.	Literary History.
1729. Birth.		**1729.** Birth of Lessing.
	1730. Evangelical movement.	
		1731. Death of Defoe.
		1732. Pope's *Essay on Man*, Epistles i and ii.
		1736. Butler's *Analogy*.
		1737. Birth of Gibbon.
		1740. Richardson's *Pamela*.
		1742. Fielding's *Joseph Andrews*. Young's *Night Thoughts*, books i-iii.
1743. Admission to Trinity College, Dublin.		
	1745. Jacobite Rebellion.	**1744.** Death of Pope.
		1745. Death of Swift.
1748. Graduation from Trinity.		**1748.** Richardson's *Clarissa Harlowe*. Smollett's *Roderick Random*.
		1749. Bolingbroke's *Idea of a Patriot King*. Fielding's *Tom Jones*. Montesquieu's *Esprit des Lois*. Birth of Goethe.
1750. Arrival in London.		**1750.** Johnson's *Rambler*.

LIFE OF BURKE.		GENERAL HISTORY.		LITERARY HISTORY.	
				1751.	Gray's *Elegy*.
					Death of Bolingbroke.
					Birth of Sheridan.
				1754.	Death of Fielding.
				1755.	Johnson's *Dictionary*.
1756.	*Vindication of Natural Society.*	1755.	French and Indian War.		
	The Sublime and Beautiful.	1756.	The Black Hole of Calcutta.		
1756-7.	Marriage to Jane Nugent.				
1757.	Account of European Settlements in America.			1757.	Birth of Blake.
	Abridgment of the History of England.				Voltaire's *Candide*.
1758.	Birth of his son, Richard Burke.			1758.	Johnson's *Idler*.
1759.	*Annual Register,* vol. I.	1759.	Capture of Quebec.	1759.	Goldsmith's *Bee*.
					Johnson's *Rasselas*.
					Sterne's *Tristram Shandy*, vols. I and II.
					Burns born.
					Schiller born.
		1760.	George the Third.		
1761.	In Ireland with Hamilton.	1762.	Bute ministry.	1762.	Hume's *History of England*, last volumes.
					Macpherson's *Ossian*.
					Rousseau's *Contrat Social*.

1763. Return to England.	1763. Grenville ministry. Proceedings against Wilkes.	
1764. Member of "The Club."		1764. Walpole's *Castle of Otranto.*
1765. Secretary to Lord Rockingham. Elected member of Parliament for Wendover.	1765. Stamp Act. Rockingham ministry.	1765. Blackstone's *Commentaries,* vol. I. Percy's *Reliques.*
1766. Repeal of Stamp Act. Grafton ministry. (The earlier part of this ministry is often called the Chatham ministry.)	1766. Repeal of Stamp Act. Grafton ministry.	1766. Goldsmith's *Vicar of Wakefield.* Lessing's *Laocoon.*
1768. Purchase of Beaconsfield.		
1769 *Observations on the Present State of the Nation.*		1769. First Letter of Junius in the *Public Advertiser.*
1770. *Thoughts on the Cause of the Present Discontents.*	1770. Boston Massacre. North ministry.	1770. Goldsmith's *Deserted Village.* Birth of Wordsworth.
1771. Agent for New York.		1771. Smollett's *Humphrey Clinker.* Death of Gray. Birth of Scott.
		1772. Birth of Coleridge.
1773. Visit to France.	1773. Boston Tea Party.	
1774. *Speech on American Taxation.* Elected member for Bristol.	1774. Boston Port Bill. Abrogation of charter of Massachusetts. First Congress at Philadelphia.	1774. Death of Goldsmith.
1775. *Speech on Conciliation.*	1775. Battles of Lexington and Bunker Hill.	1775. Johnson's *Taxation No Tyranny.* Birth of Lamb.

Life of Burke.	General History.	Literary History.
	1776. Declaration of Independence.	1776. Gibbon's *Decline and Fall of the Roman Empire*, vol. I. Paine's *Common Sense*. Adam Smith's *Wealth of Nations*.
1777. *Address to the King. Letter to the Sheriffs of Bristol.*		
	1778. Death of Chatham.	1778. Frances Burney's *Evelina*.
		1779. Johnson's *Lives of the Poets*.
1780. *Speech on Economical Reform.* Loss of seat at Bristol.	1780. Lord George Gordon riots.	
1781. Member for Malton.	1781. Surrender of Cornwallis.	
1782. Paymaster of the Forces.	1782. Second Rockingham ministry. Death of Rockingham. Shelburne ministry.	1782. Birth of Daniel Webster.
1783. *Speech on Fox's East India Bill.*	1783. Coalition ministry.	1783. Birth of Washington Irving.
	1784. Pitt ministry.	1784. Death of Johnson.
1785. *Speech on the Nabob of Arcot's Debts.*		1785. Cowper's *Task*.
1786. Beginning of the proceedings against Hastings.		1786. Burns's *Poems Chiefly in the Scottish Dialect.*
	1787. Framing of Constitution of the United States.	1788. Byron born.
	1789. Beginning of French Revolution. Washington first president.	1789. Blake's *Songs of Innocence.*

1790. *Reflections on the Revolution in France.*		
1791. Breach with Fox and Sheridan. *Letter to a Member of the National Assembly.*		1791. Boswell's *Life of Johnson.*
1792. *Appeal from the New to the Old Whigs. Thoughts on French Affairs.*	1792. Suspension of King Louis XIV.	1792. Birth of Shelley. Paine's *Rights of Man.* Paine's *Age of Reason.*
1793. *Observations on the Conduct of the Minority. Remarks on the Policy of the Allies.*	1793. Execution of the king. Reign of Terror. War declared by France against England, Holland and Spain.	
1794. Closing speeches in the trial of Hastings. Retirement from Parliament. Death of his son Richard.	1794. Fall of Robespierre.	
1795. *Thoughts and Details on Scarcity. Letter to a Noble Lord.*	1795. Bonaparte's Italian campaign. Constitution of the year III. Rising of the 13th Vendémiaire (Oct. 4) put down by Bonaparte.	1795. Birth of Carlyle. Birth of Keats.
1796. *First two Letters on a Regicide Peace.*		
1797. Death July 9.	1797. John Adams president.	1797. The *Anti-Jacobin.*

BIBLIOGRAPHICAL NOTE.

There is so much material of interest in the study of the *Speech on Conciliation* and of Burke's writings and speeches in general that a complete bibliography is out of the question in this volume. The books named below are, however, the more important. Most of them are specifically referred to in the Introduction or the Notes.

The most accessible American edition of Burke's *Works* is that in twelve volumes, Little, Brown & Company, Boston, 1894. The *Account of the European Settlements in America* is not in this edition, though it was in an earlier edition published by the same firm, and now rather hard to get. The *European Settlements* may now and then be bought in one of the two-volume editions published in London in the last century. There are several English editions of Burke, of which that by Bohn, 1893, in eight volumes, is on the whole the best. No edition contains Burke's contributions to the *Annual Register*, which are often difficult to identify. No edition contains more than a fraction of the many fragmentary reports of his speeches scattered through the *Parliamentary History* and other collections. Indeed, he himself prepared for press but very few speeches and left notes on but few more. His *Correspondence* was published at London in four volumes in 1844.

The *Speech on Conciliation* is printed with annotations in the following editions : C. A. Goodrich, *Select British Eloquence*, Harpers, New York ; E. J. Payne, Burke's *Select Works*, Clarendon Press, 1892, vol. I ; F. G. Selby, Burke's *Speeches*, Macmillan, New York, 1895 ; A. S. Cook, *Speech on Conciliation*, Longmans, New York, 1896 ; Henry Morley, *Universal Library*, London, 1892. The volume of Perry's *Selections from Burke*, though it does not contain the *Speech on Conciliation*, presents well-chosen specimens of the whole range of Burke's writing and oratory.

The above-mentioned annotated editions, except that of the *Universal Library*, devote more or less space to an account of Burke's life and a criticism of his style. The best life, however, is that by John Morley in the *English Men of Letters*. Morley has also considered Burke's statesmanship in an earlier work, *Edmund Burke : a Historical Study*, London,

1869. A more detailed biography is that of James Prior, two volumes, London, 1854. A later and better work is Thomas MacKnight's *History of the Life and Times of Edmund Burke*, three volumes, London, 1858. The life in the *Dictionary of National Biography* furnishes many references and a bibliography. Several other short accounts of Burke are also valuable: those in the *Annual Register* for 1797 and 1798; J. R. Green's in chapter X of the *History of the English People;* H. T. Buckle's in volume I of his *History of Civilization in Europe;* Sir Joseph Napier's lecture on Burke before the Young Men's Christian Association of Dublin, in 1862; Lord Brougham's sketch in his *Statesmen of the Time of George the Third;* Augustine Birrell's in *Obiter Dicta*, Second Series, New York, 1887; F. D. Maurice's lecture on Burke in *Friendship of Books*, 1874; and Woodrow Wilson's essay, *The Interpreter of English Liberty*, in the volume *Mere Literature*, 1896. In the *Proceedings* of the American Antiquarian Society for October, 1893, Calvin Stebbins discusses Burke's agency for the province of New York.

Vivid pictures of the time, and often of Burke himself, are presented in Boswell's *Life of Johnson*, Horace Walpole's *Letters* and *Memoirs*, Madame D'Arblay's *Diary and Letters*, Jesse's *George Selwyn and His Contemporaries* and *Memoirs of George the Third*, Wraxall's *Historical and Posthumous Memoirs*, the *Rockingham Memoirs*, the *Grenville Papers*, Lord Chesterfield's *Letters*, Thackeray's *Four Georges* and *English Humorists*, and Macaulay's essays on *Warren Hastings* and *Chatham*. There is also an interesting passage on Burke in Macaulay's *Essay on Bacon*.

Of the English historians who deal with the period of the *Speech on Conciliation*, Adolphus, in the *History of England from the Accession to the Decease of George the Third*, is prejudiced against the Americans; W. E. H. Lecky, in the *History of England in the Eighteenth Century*, is not an ardent admirer of republican institutions, but he is fair in his statements; J. R. Green, in *History of the English People*, and H. T. Buckle, in *History of Civilization in Europe*, are more decidedly pro-American in tone; Leslie Stephen, in the *History of English Thought in the Eighteenth Century*, treats more especially the development of political ideas. Goldwin Smith's residence in Canada has given him a more intimate knowledge of America than most Englishmen possess, and accordingly in his *United States* he has given perhaps the best succinct account written by an Englishman. Of the Americans Bancroft is decidedly unfair to England; E. B. Andrews, in his *History of the United States*, and John Fiske, in the *American Revolution*, are both brief and impartial.

Many details which are omitted from the regular histories but which form the basis for the generalizations of history may be found in the *Par-*

liamentary History, the *Journals of the American Congress*, the *Statutes at Large*, and the *Annual Register*.   Low and Pulling's *Dictionary of English History* and J. F. Jameson's *Dictionary of United States History, 1492–1894*, Boston, 1894, are very convenient for reference.

The attitude of Burke's contemporaries may be studied in the speeches of Chatham and of Fox, in the *Letters of Junius*, in the writings of Franklin, and in the innumerable political tracts of the time, such as Dr. Johnson's *Taxation No Tyranny*, Dean Tucker's *Four Tracts on Political and Commercial Subjects*, Thomas Paine's *Common Sense*, and Richard Price's *Civil Liberty*.

THE

S P E E C H

OF

EDMUND BURKE, Eſq;

ON

MOVING HIS RESOLUTIONS

FOR

CONCILIATION with the COLONIES,

MARCH 22, 1775.

L O N D O N:

PRINTED FOR J. DODSLEY.

MDCCLXXV.

SPEECH ON

CONCILIATION WITH AMERICA.

I HOPE, Sir, that notwithstanding the austerity of the Chair, your good nature will incline you to some degree of indulgence towards human frailty. You will not think it unnatural that those who have an object depending which strongly engages their hopes and fears should be somewhat inclined to superstition. As I came into the House, full of anxiety about the event of my motion, I found, to my infinite surprise, that the grand penal bill by which we had passed sentence on the trade and sustenance of America is to be returned to us from the other House. I do confess, I could not help looking on this event as a fortunate omen. I look upon it as a sort of providential favor by which we are put once more in possession of our deliberative capacity, upon a business so very questionable in its nature, so very uncertain in its issue. By the return of this bill, which seemed to have taken its flight forever, we are at this very instant nearly as free to choose a plan for our American government as we were on the first day of the session. If, Sir, we incline to the side of conciliation, we are not at all embarrassed (unless we please to make ourselves so) by any incongruous mixture of coercion and restraint. We are therefore called upon, as it were by a superior warning voice, again to attend to America; to attend to the whole of it together; and to review the subject with an unusual degree of care and calmness.

Surely it is an awful subject, or there is none so on this side of the grave.   When I first had the honor of a seat in this House, the affairs of that continent pressed themselves upon us as the most important and most delicate object of
5 parliamentary attention.   My little share in this great deliberation oppressed me.   I found myself a partaker in a very high trust ; and having no sort of reason to rely on the strength of my natural abilities for the proper execution of that trust, I was obliged to take more than common pains
10 to instruct myself in everything which relates to our colonies.   I was not less under the necessity of forming some fixed ideas concerning the general policy of the British Empire.   Something of this sort seemed to be indispensable, in order, amidst so vast a fluctuation of passions
15 and opinions, to concentre my thoughts, to ballast my conduct, to preserve me from being blown about by every wind of fashionable doctrine.   I really did not think it safe or manly to have fresh principles to seek upon every fresh mail which should arrive from America.

20   At that period I had the fortune to find myself in perfect concurrence with a large majority in this House.   Bowing under that high authority, and penetrated with the sharpness and strength of that early impression, I have continued ever since, without the least deviation, in my original senti-
25 ments.   Whether this be owing to an obstinate perseverance in error, or to a religious adherence to what appears to me truth and reason, it is in your equity to judge.

Sir, Parliament having an enlarged view of objects, made, during this interval, more frequent changes in their
30 sentiments and their conduct than could be justified in a particular person upon the contracted scale of private information.   But though I do not hazard anything approaching to a censure on the motives of former Parliaments to all those alterations, one fact is undoubted, — that

under them the state of America has been kept in continual agitation. Everything administered as remedy to the public complaint, if it did not produce, was at least followed by, an heightening of the distemper; until by a variety of experiments that important country has been brought into her present situation — a situation which I will not miscall, which I dare not name, which I scarcely know how to comprehend in the terms of any description.

In this posture, Sir, things stood at the beginning of the session. About that time a worthy member, of great parliamentary experience, who in the year 1766 filled the Chair of the American Committee with much ability, took me aside and, lamenting the present aspect of our politics, told me things were come to such a pass that our former methods of proceeding in the House would be no longer tolerated; that the public tribunal (never too indulgent to a long and unsuccessful opposition) would now scrutinize our conduct with unusual severity; that the very vicissitudes and shiftings of ministerial measures, instead of convicting their authors of inconstancy and want of system, would be taken as an occasion of charging us with a predetermined discontent which nothing could satisfy, whilst we accused every measure of vigor as cruel, and every proposal of lenity as weak and irresolute. The public, he said, would not have patience to see us play the game out with our adversaries; we must produce our hand: it would be expected that those who for many years had been active in such affairs should show that they had formed some clear and decided idea of the principles of colony government; and were capable of drawing out something like a platform of the ground which might be laid for future and permanent tranquillity.

I felt the truth of what my honorable friend represented; but I felt my situation too. His application might have

been made with far greater propriety to many other gentlemen.   No man was indeed ever better disposed, or worse
qualified, for such an undertaking than myself.   Though I
gave so far into his opinion that I immediately threw my
5 thoughts into a sort of parliamentary form, I was by no
means equally ready to produce them.   It generally argues
some degree of natural impotence of mind, or some want of
knowledge of the world, to hazard plans of government,
except from a seat of authority.   Propositions are made,
10 not only ineffectually, but somewhat disreputably, when the
minds of men are not properly disposed for their reception ;
and for my part, I am not ambitious of ridicule, not absolutely a candidate for disgrace.

Besides, Sir, to speak the plain truth, I have in general
15 no very exalted opinion of the virtue of paper government,
nor of any politics in which the plan is to be wholly separated from the execution.   But when I saw that anger and
violence prevailed every day more and more, and that things
were hastening towards an incurable alienation of our colo-
20 nies, I confess my caution gave way.   I felt this as one of
those few moments in which decorum yields to an higher
duty.   Public calamity is a mighty leveller ; and there are
occasions when any, even the slightest, chance of doing
good must be laid hold on, even by the most inconsiderable
25 person.

To restore order and repose to an empire so great and so
distracted as ours, is, merely in the attempt, an undertaking
that would ennoble the flights of the highest genius and
obtain pardon for the efforts of the meanest understanding.
30 Struggling a good while with these thoughts, by degrees I
felt myself more firm.   I derived, at length, some confidence
from what in other circumstances usually produces timidity.
I grew less anxious, even from the idea of my own insignificance.   For judging of what you are by what you ought to

be, I persuaded myself that you would not reject a reasonable proposition, because it had nothing but its reason to
recommend it. On the other hand, being totally destitute
of all shadow of influence, natural or adventitious, I was
very sure that if my proposition were futile or dangerous,   5
if it were weakly conceived or improperly timed, there was
nothing exterior to it, of power to awe, dazzle or delude
you. You will see it just as it is, and you will treat it just
as it deserves.

  The proposition is peace. Not peace through the medium   10
of war; not peace to be hunted through the labyrinth of
intricate and endless negotiations; not peace to arise out
of universal discord fomented from principle in all parts
of the empire; not peace to depend on the juridical determination of perplexing questions, or the precise marking   15
the shadowy boundaries of a complex government. It is
simple peace, sought in its natural course and its ordinary
haunts. It is peace sought in the spirit of peace, and
laid in principles purely pacific. I propose, by removing
the ground of the difference, and by restoring the *former*   20
unsuspecting confidence of the colonies in the mother country, to
give permanent satisfaction to your people; and (far from a
scheme of ruling by discord) to reconcile them to each other
in the same act and by the bond of the very same interest
which reconciles them to British government.   25

  My idea is nothing more. Refined policy ever has been
the parent of confusion; and ever will be so, as long as the
world endures. Plain good intention, which is as easily
discovered at the first view as fraud is surely detected at
last, is, let me say, of no mean force in the government of   30
mankind. Genuine simplicity of heart is an healing and
cementing principle. My plan, therefore, being formed
upon the most simple grounds imaginable, may disappoint
some people when they hear it. It has nothing to recom-

mend it to the pruriency of curious ears. There is nothing
at all new and captivating in it. It has nothing of the
splendor of the project which has been lately laid upon your
table by the noble lord in the blue ribbon. It does not
5 propose to fill your lobby with squabbling colony agents,
who will require the interposition of your mace at every
instant to keep the peace amongst them. It does not in-
stitute a magnificent auction of finance, where captivated
provinces come to general ransom by bidding against each
10 other, until you knock down the hammer, and determine a
proportion of payments beyond all the powers of algebra to
equalize and settle.

The plan which I shall presume to suggest derives, however, one great advantage from the proposition and registry
15 of that noble lord's project. The idea of conciliation is
admissible. First, the House, in accepting the resolution
moved by the noble lord, has admitted, notwithstanding the
menacing front of our address, notwithstanding our heavy
bill of pains and penalties, that we do not think ourselves
20 precluded from all ideas of free grace and bounty.

The House has gone farther : it has declared conciliation
admissible, *previous* to any submission on the part of America. It has even shot a good deal beyond that mark, and
has admitted that the complaints of our former mode of
25 exerting the right of taxation were not wholly unfounded.
That right thus exerted is allowed to have had something rep-
rehensible in it, something unwise or something grievous ;
since, in the midst of our heat and resentment, we of ourselves have proposed a capital alteration ; and, in order to
30 get rid of what seemed so very exceptionable, have instituted
a mode that is altogether new, — one that is, indeed, wholly
alien from all the ancient methods and forms of Parliament.

The *principle* of this proceeding is large enough for my
purpose. The means proposed by the noble lord for carry-

ing his ideas into execution, I think, indeed, are very indif-
ferently suited to the end; and this I shall endeavor to
show you before I sit down. But, for the present, I take
my ground on the admitted principle. I mean to give peace.
Peace implies reconciliation; and where there has been a 5
material dispute, reconciliation does in a manner always
imply concession on the one part or on the other. In this
state of things I make no difficulty in affirming that the
proposal ought to originate from us. Great and acknowledged force is not impaired, either in effect or in opinion, 10
by an unwillingness to exert itself. The superior power
may offer peace with honor and with safety. Such an offer
from such a power will be attributed to magnanimity. But
the concessions of the weak are the concessions of fear.
When such a one is disarmed, he is wholly at the mercy of 15
his superior; and he loses forever that time and those
chances which, as they happen to all men, are the strength
and resources of all inferior power.

The capital leading questions on which you must this
day decide are these two: first, whether you ought to con- 20
cede; and secondly, what your concession ought to be.
On the first of these questions we have gained (as I have
just taken the liberty of observing to you) some ground.
But I am sensible that a good deal more is still to be done.
Indeed, Sir, to enable us to determine both on the one and 25
the other of these great questions with a firm and precise
judgment, I think it may be necessary to consider distinctly
the true nature and the peculiar circumstances of the object
which we have before us: because after all our struggle,
whether we will or not, we must govern America according 30
to that nature and to those circumstances, and not according
to our own imaginations, not according to abstract ideas of
right; by no means according to mere general theories of
government, the resort to which appears to me in our pres-

ent situation no better than arrant trifling. I shall therefore endeavor, with your leave, to lay before you some of the
most material of these circumstances in as full and as clear
a manner as I am able to state them.

5   The first thing that we have to consider with regard to
the nature of the object is the number of people in the
colonies. I have taken for some years a good deal of pains
on that point. I can by no calculation justify myself in
placing the number below two millions of inhabitants of our
10 own European blood and color ; besides at least 500,000
others, who form no inconsiderable part of the strength and
opulence of the whole. This, Sir, is, I believe, about the
true number. There is no occasion to exaggerate where
plain truth is of so much weight and importance. But
15 whether I put the present numbers too high or too low is a
matter of little moment. Such is the strength with which
population shoots in that part of the world, that, state the
numbers as high as we will, whilst the dispute continues,
the exaggeration ends. Whilst we are discussing any given
20 magnitude, they are grown to it. Whilst we spend our time
in deliberating on the mode of governing two millions, we
shall find we have millions more to manage. Your children
do not grow faster from infancy to manhood than they
spread from families to communities, and from villages to
25 nations.

I put this consideration of the present and the growing
numbers in the front of our deliberation ; because, Sir, this
consideration will make it evident to a blunter discernment
than yours, that no partial, narrow, contracted, pinched,
30 occasional system will be at all suitable to such an object.
It will show you that it is not to be considered as one of
those *minima* which are out of the eye and consideration of
the law ; not a paltry excrescence of the state ; not a mean
dependent, who may be neglected with little damage and

provoked with little danger.   It will prove that some degree
of care and caution is required in the handling such an
object; it will show that you ought not, in reason, to trifle
with so large a mass of the interests and feelings of the
human race.   You could at no time do so without guilt; 5
and be assured you will not be able to do it long with
impunity.

But the population of this country, the great and growing
population, though a very important consideration, will lose
much of its weight, if not combined with other circum- 10
stances.   The commerce of your colonies is out of all proportion beyond the numbers of the people.   This ground of
their commerce, indeed, has been trod some days ago, and
with great ability, by a distinguished person at your bar.
This gentleman, after thirty-five years, — it is so long since 15
he first appeared at the same place to plead for the commerce of Great Britain, — has come again before you to
plead the same cause, without any other effect of time
than that to the fire of imagination and extent of erudition,
which even then marked him as one of the first literary 20
characters of his age, he has added a consummate knowledge in the commercial interest of his country, formed by a
long course of enlightened and discriminating experience.

Sir, I should be inexcusable in coming after such a person
with any detail, if a great part of the members who now fill 25
the House had not the misfortune to be absent when he
appeared at your bar.   Besides, Sir, I propose to take the
matter at periods of time somewhat different from his.
There is, if I mistake not, a point of view from whence, if
you will look at this subject, it is impossible that it should 30
not make an impression upon you.

I have in my hand two accounts : one a comparative state
of the export trade of England to its colonies, as it stood in
the year 1704, and as it stood in the year 1772 ; the other

a state of the export trade of this country to its colonies alone, as it stood in 1772, compared with the whole trade of England to all parts of the world (the colonies included) in the year 1704. They are from good vouchers : the latter period from the accounts on your table ; the earlier from an original manuscript of Davenant, who first established the Inspector-General's office, which has been even since his time so abundant a source of parliamentary information.

The export trade to the colonies consists of three great branches : the African, which, terminating almost wholly in the colonies, must be put to the account of their commerce ; the West Indian ; and the North American. All these are so interwoven that the attempt to separate them would tear to pieces the contexture of the whole; and if not entirely destroy, would very much depreciate, the value of all the parts. I therefore consider these three denominations to be, what in effect they are, one trade.

The trade to the colonies, taken on the export side, at the beginning of this century, that is, in the year 1704, stood thus : —

Exports to North America and the West Indies, £483,265
To Africa   86,665
                                   ————————
                                    £569,930

In the year 1772, which I take as a middle year between the highest and lowest of those lately laid on your table, the account was as follows : —

To North America and the West Indies . . £4,791,734
To Africa   866,398
To which if you add the export trade from
  Scotland, which had in 1704 no existence   364,000
                                           ————————
                                          £6,022,132

From five hundred and odd thousand it has grown to six millions. It has increased no less than twelvefold. This is

the state of the colony trade, as compared with itself at
these two periods within this century; and this is matter
for meditation. But this is not all. Examine my second
account. See how the export trade to the colonies alone in
1772 stood in the other point of view, that is, as compared to   5
the whole trade of England in 1704 : —

The whole export trade of England, including
  that to the colonies, in 1704 . . . . £6,509,000
Export to the colonies alone in 1772 . . . 6,024,000
                                              —————————
                      Difference £485,000   10

The trade with America alone is now within less than
£500,000 of being equal to what this great commercial
nation, England, carried on at the beginning of this century
with the whole world! If I had taken the largest year of
those on your table, it would rather have exceeded. But, it   15
will be said, is not this American trade an unnatural protu-
berance that has drawn the juices from the rest of the body?
The reverse. It is the very food that has nourished every
other part into its present magnitude. Our general trade
has been greatly augmented, and augmented more or less in   20
almost every part to which it ever extended, but with this
material difference : that of the six millions which in the
beginning of the century constituted the whole mass of our
export commerce, the colony trade was but one-twelfth part ;
it is now (as a part of sixteen millions) considerably more   25
than a third of the whole. This is the relative proportion
of the importance of the colonies at these two periods : and
all reasoning concerning our mode of treating them must
have this proportion as its basis ; or it is a reasoning weak,
rotten and sophistical.   30

Mr. Speaker, I cannot prevail on myself to hurry over
this great consideration. It is good for us to be here. We
stand where we have an immense view of what is, and what

is past.   Clouds, indeed, and darkness rest upon the future.
Let us, however, before we descend from this noble eminence, reflect that this growth of our national prosperity has
happened within the short period of the life of man.   It has
5 happened within sixty-eight years.   There are those alive
whose memory might touch the two extremities.   For
instance, my Lord Bathurst might remember all the stages
of the progress.   He was in 1704 of an age at least to be
made to comprehend such things.   He was then old enough
10 *acta parentum jam legere, et quae sit poterit cognoscere virtus.*
Suppose, Sir, that the angel of this auspicious youth, fore-
seeing the many virtues which made him one of the most
amiable, as he is one of the most fortunate, men of his age,
had opened to him in vision, that when in the fourth gener-
15 ation the third prince of the House of Brunswick had sat
twelve years on the throne of that nation which (by the
happy issue of moderate and healing counsels) was to be
made Great Britain, he should see his son, Lord Chancellor
of England, turn back the current of hereditary dignity to its
20 fountain, and raise him to an higher rank of peerage, whilst
he enriched the family with a new one; — if, amidst these
bright and happy scenes of domestic honor and prosperity,
that angel should have drawn up the curtain and unfolded
the rising glories of his country, and, whilst he was gazing
25 with admiration on the then commercial grandeur of England,
the genius should point out to him a little speck, scarcely
visible in the mass of the national interest, a small seminal
principle rather than a formed body, and should tell him, —
"Young man, there is America, which at this day serves
30 for little more than to amuse you with stories of savage men
and uncouth manners; yet shall, before you taste of death,
show itself equal to the whole of that commerce which now
attracts the envy of the world.   Whatever England has been
growing to by a progressive increase of improvement,

brought in by varieties of people, by succession of civilizing conquests and civilizing settlements in a series of seventeen hundred years, you shall see as much added to her by America in the course of a single life!" If this state of his country had been foretold to him, would it not require all the sanguine credulity of youth and all the fervid glow of enthusiasm to make him believe it? Fortunate man, he has lived to see it! Fortunate indeed, if he lives to see nothing that shall vary the prospect and cloud the setting of his day!

Excuse me, Sir, if, turning from such thoughts, I resume this comparative view once more. You have seen it on a large scale; look at it on a small one. I will point out to your attention a particular instance of it in the single province of Pennsylvania. In the year 1704 that province called for £11,459 in value of your commodities, native and foreign. This was the whole. What did it demand in 1772? Why, nearly fifty times as much; for in that year the export to Pennsylvania was £507,909, nearly equal to the export to all the colonies together in the first period.

I choose, Sir, to enter into these minute and particular details; because generalities, which in all other cases are apt to heighten and raise the subject, have here a tendency to sink it. When we speak of the commerce with our colonies, fiction lags after truth, invention is unfruitful, and imagination cold and barren.

So far, Sir, as to the importance of the object in the view of its commerce, as concerned in the exports from England. If I were to detail the imports, I could show how many enjoyments they procure which deceive the burden of life, how many materials which invigorate the springs of national industry, and extend and animate every part of our foreign and domestic commerce. This would be a curious subject indeed,—but I must prescribe bounds to myself in a matter so vast and various.

I pass, therefore, to the colonies in another point of view, — their agriculture. This they have prosecuted with such a spirit that, besides feeding plentifully their own growing multitude, their annual export of grain, comprehending rice,

5 has some years ago exceeded a million in value. Of their last harvest, I am persuaded, they will export much more. At the beginning of the century some of these colonies imported corn from the mother country. For some time past the Old World has been fed from the New. The scarcity

10 which you have felt would have been a desolating famine, if this child of your old age, with a true filial piety, with a Roman charity, had not put the full breast of its youthful exuberance to the mouth of its exhausted parent.

As to the wealth which the colonies have drawn from the

15 sea by their fisheries, you had all that matter fully opened at your bar. You surely thought those acquisitions of value, for they seemed even to excite your envy; and yet the spirit by which that enterprising employment has been exercised ought rather, in my opinion, to have raised your esteem and

20 admiration. And pray, Sir, what in the world is equal to it? Pass by the other parts, and look at the manner in which the people of New England have of late carried on the whale fishery. Whilst we follow them among the tumbling mountains of ice, and behold them penetrating into

25 the deepest frozen recesses of Hudson Bay and Davis Strait, whilst we are looking for them beneath the Arctic Circle, we hear that they have pierced into the opposite region of polar cold, that they are at the antipodes and engaged under the frozen Serpent of the south. Falkland

30 Island, which seemed too remote and romantic an object for the grasp of national ambition, is but a stage and resting-place in the progress of their victorious industry. Nor is the equinoctial heat more discouraging to them than the accumulated winter of both the poles. We know that whilst

some of them draw the line and strike the harpoon on the coast of Africa, others run the longitude and pursue their gigantic game along the coast of Brazil. No sea but what is vexed by their fisheries. No climate that is not witness to their toils. Neither the perseverance of Holland nor the activity of France nor the dexterous and firm sagacity of English enterprise ever carried this most perilous mode of hardy industry to the extent to which it has been pushed by this recent people — a people who are still, as it were, but in the gristle, and not yet hardened into the bone of manhood. When I contemplate these things; when I know that the colonies in general owe little or nothing to any care of ours, and that they are not squeezed into this happy form by the constraints of watchful and suspicious government, but that through a wise and salutary neglect a generous nature has been suffered to take her own way to perfection ; — when I reflect upon these effects, when I see how profitable they have been to us, I feel all the pride of power sink, and all presumption in the wisdom of human contrivances melt and die away within me. My rigor relents. I pardon something to the spirit of liberty.

I am sensible, Sir, that all which I have asserted in my detail is admitted in the gross, but that quite a different conclusion is drawn from it. America, gentlemen say, is a noble object ; it is an object well worth fighting for. Certainly it is, if fighting a people be the best way of gaining them. Gentlemen in this respect will be led to their choice of means by their complexions and their habits. Those who understand the military art will of course have some predilection for it. Those who wield the thunder of the state may have more confidence in the efficacy of arms. But I confess, possibly for want of this knowledge, my opinion is much more in favor of prudent management than of force, — considering force not as an odious, but a feeble, instrument for preserving a people so numerous, so active, so growing, so spirited as this, in a profitable and subordinate connection with us.

First, Sir, permit me to observe that the use of force alone is but *temporary*. It may subdue for a moment, but it does not remove the necessity of subduing again : and a nation is not governed which is perpetually to be conquered.

My next objection is its *uncertainty*. Terror is not always the effect of force ; and an armament is not a victory. If you do not succeed, you are without resource : for conciliation failing, force remains ; but force failing, no further hope of reconciliation is left. Power and authority are sometimes bought by kindness ; but they can never be begged as alms by an impoverished and defeated violence.

A further objection to force is that you *impair the object* by your very endeavors to preserve it. The thing you fought for is not the thing which you recover ; but depreciated, sunk, wasted and consumed in the contest. Nothing less will content me than *whole America*. I do not choose to consume its strength along with our own ; because in all parts it is the British strength that I consume. I do not choose to be caught by a foreign enemy at the end of this exhausting conflict ; and still less in the midst of it. I may escape ; but I can make no insurance against such an event. Let me add that I do not choose wholly to break the American spirit ; because it is the spirit that has made the country.

Lastly, we have no sort of *experience* in favor of force as an instrument in the rule of our colonies. Their growth and their utility has been owing to methods altogether different. Our ancient indulgence has been said to be pursued to a fault. It may be so ; but we know, if feeling is evidence, that our fault was more tolerable than our attempt to mend it, and our sin far more salutary than our penitence.

These, Sir, are my reasons for not entertaining that high opinion of untried force, by which many gentlemen, for whose sentiments in other particulars I have great respect, seem to be so greatly captivated. But there is still behind a third consideration concerning this object, which serves to determine my opinion on the sort of policy which ought to be pursued in the management of America, even more than its population and its commerce : I mean its *temper and character*.

In this character of the Americans a love of freedom is the predominating feature which marks and distinguishes the whole : and as an ardent is always a jealous affection, your colonies become suspicious, restive and untractable, whenever they see the least attempt to wrest from them by force or shuffle from them by chicane what they think the only advantage worth living for. This fierce spirit of liberty is stronger in the English colonies probably than in any other people of the earth ; and this from a great variety of powerful causes, which, to understand the true temper of their minds and the direction which this spirit takes, it will not be amiss to lay open somewhat more largely.

First, the people of the colonies are descendants of Englishmen. England, Sir, is a nation which still, I hope, respects, and formerly adored, her freedom. The colonists emigrated from you when this part of your character was most predominant ; and they took this bias and direction the moment they parted from your hands. They are therefore not only devoted to liberty, but to liberty according to English ideas and on English principles. Abstract liberty, like other mere abstractions, is not to be found. Liberty inheres in some sensible object ; and every nation has formed to itself some favorite point, which by way of eminence becomes the criterion of their happiness. It happened, you know, Sir, that the great contests for freedom in

this country were from the earliest times chiefly upon the question of taxing. Most of the contests in the ancient commonwealths turned primarily on the right of election of magistrates or on the balance among the several orders of
5 the state. The question of money was not with them so immediate. But in England it was otherwise. On this point of taxes the ablest pens and most eloquent tongues have been exercised, the greatest spirits have acted and suffered. In order to give the fullest satisfaction concern-
10 ing the importance of this point, it was not only necessary for those who in argument defended the excellence of the English Constitution to insist on this privilege of granting money as a dry point of fact, and to prove that the right had been acknowledged in ancient parchments and blind
15 usages to reside in a certain body called a House of Commons. They went much further: they attempted to prove, and they succeeded, that in theory it ought to be so, from the particular nature of the House of Commons as an immediate representative of the people, whether the old records
20 had delivered this oracle or not. They took infinite pains to inculcate as a fundamental principle, that in all monarchies the people must in effect themselves, mediately or immediately, possess the power of granting their own money, or no shadow of liberty could subsist. The colonies draw
25 from you, as with their life-blood, these ideas and principles. Their love of liberty, as with you, fixed and attached on this specific point of taxing. Liberty might be safe or might be endangered in twenty other particulars without their being much pleased or alarmed. Here they felt its pulse; and as
30 they found that beat, they thought themselves sick or sound. I do not say whether they were right or wrong in applying your general arguments to their own case. It is not easy, indeed, to make a monopoly of theorems and corollaries. The fact is that they did thus apply those general argu-

ments ; and your mode of governing them, whether through lenity or indolence, through wisdom or mistake, confirmed them in the imagination that they, as well as you, had an interest in these common principles.

They were further confirmed in this pleasing error by the form of their provincial legislative assemblies. Their governments are popular in an high degree : some are merely popular ; in all the popular representative is the most weighty ; and this share of the people in their ordinary government never fails to inspire them with lofty sentiments and with a strong aversion from whatever tends to deprive them of their chief importance.

If anything were wanting to this necessary operation of the form of government, religion would have given it a complete effect. Religion, always a principle of energy, in this new people is no way worn out or impaired ; and their mode of professing it is also one main cause of this free spirit. The people are Protestants, and of that kind which is the most adverse to all implicit submission of mind and opinion. This is a persuasion not only favorable to liberty, but built upon it. I do not think, Sir, that the reason of this averseness in the dissenting churches from all that looks like absolute government is so much to be sought in their religious tenets as in their history. Every one knows that the Roman Catholic religion is at least coeval with most of the governments where it prevails ; that it has generally gone hand in hand with them, and received great favor and every kind of support from authority. The Church of England too was formed from her cradle under the nursing care of regular government. But the dissenting interests have sprung up in direct opposition to all the ordinary powers of the world, and could justify that opposition only on a strong claim to natural liberty. Their very existence depended on the powerful and unremitted assertion of that claim. All Protestantism, even the most cold and passive, is a sort of dissent. But the religion most prevalent in our northern colonies is a refinement on the principle of resistance : it is the dissidence of dissent and the Protestantism 5 of the Protestant religion. This religion, under a variety of denominations agreeing in nothing but in the communion of the spirit of liberty, is predominant in most of the northern provinces, where the Church of England, notwithstanding its legal rights, is in reality no more than a sort of private 10 sect, not composing most probably the tenth of the people. The colonists left England when this spirit was high, and in the emigrants was the highest of all ; and even that stream of foreigners which has been constantly flowing into these colonies has, for the greatest part, been composed of dis- 15 senters from the establishments of their several countries, and have brought with them a temper and character far from alien to that of the people with whom they mixed.

Sir, I can perceive by their manner that some gentlemen object to the latitude of this description, because in the 20 southern colonies the Church of England forms a large body and has a regular establishment. It is certainly true. There is, however, a circumstance attending these colonies, which, in my opinion, fully counterbalances this difference and makes the spirit of liberty still more high and haughty 25 than in those to the northward. It is, that in Virginia and the Carolinas they have a vast multitude of slaves. Where this is the case in any part of the world, those who are free are by far the most proud and jealous of their freedom. Freedom is to them not only an enjoyment, but a kind of 30 rank and privilege. Not seeing there that freedom, as in countries where it is a common blessing and as broad and general as the air, may be united with much abject toil, with great misery, with all the exterior of servitude, liberty looks, amongst them, like something that is more noble and liberal.

I do not mean, Sir, to commend the superior morality of this sentiment, which has at least as much pride as virtue in it ; but I cannot alter the nature of man. The fact is so ; and these people of the southern colonies are much more strongly and with a higher and more stubborn spirit 5 attached to liberty than those to the northward. Such were all the ancient commonwealths ; such were our Gothic ancestors ; such in our days were the Poles ; and such will be all masters of slaves, who are not slaves themselves. In such a people the haughtiness of domination combines with 10 the spirit of freedom, fortifies it, and renders it invincible.

Permit me, Sir, to add another circumstance in our colonies, which contributes no mean part towards the growth and effect of this untractable spirit: I mean their education. In no country perhaps in the world is the law so general a 15 study. The profession itself is numerous and powerful, and in most provinces it takes the lead. The greater number of the deputies sent to the Congress were lawyers. But all who read (and most do read) endeavor to obtain some smattering in that science. I have been told by an eminent 20 bookseller that in no branch of his business, after tracts of popular devotion, were so many books as those on the law exported to the plantations. The colonists have now fallen into the way of printing them for their own use. I hear that they have sold nearly as many of Blackstone's *Commen-* 25 *taries* in America as in England. General Gage marks out this disposition very particularly in a letter on your table. He states that all the people in his government are lawyers or smatterers in law ; and that in Boston they have been enabled by successful chicane wholly to evade many parts 30 of one of your capital penal constitutions. The smartness of debate will say that this knowledge ought to teach them more clearly the rights of legislature, their obligations to obedience and the penalties of rebellion. All this is mighty

well.   But my honorable and learned friend on the floor,
who condescends to mark what I say for animadversion,
will disdain that ground.   He has heard, as well as I, that
when great honors and great emoluments do not win over
5 this knowledge to the service of the state, it is a formidable
adversary to government.   If the spirit be not tamed and
broken by these happy methods, it is stubborn and litigious.
Abeunt studia in mores.   This study renders men acute,
inquisitive, dexterous, prompt in attack, ready in defence,
10 full of resources.   In other countries the people, more simple and of a less mercurial cast, judge of an ill principle in
government only by an actual grievance ; here they antici-
pate the evil and judge of the pressure of the grievance by
the badness of the principle.   They augur misgovernment
15 at a distance and snuff the approach of tyranny in every
tainted breeze.

The last cause of this disobedient spirit in the colonies is
hardly less powerful than the rest, as it is not merely moral,
but laid deep in the natural constitution of things.   Three
20 thousand miles of ocean lie between you and them.   No
contrivance can prevent the effect of this distance in weak-
ening government.   Seas roll and months pass between
the order and the execution ; and the want of a speedy
explanation of a single point is enough to defeat a whole
25 system.   You have, indeed, winged ministers of vengeance,
who carry your bolts in their pounces to the remotest verge
of the sea.   But there a power steps in that limits the
arrogance of raging passions and furious elements, and
says, "So far shalt thou go, and no farther."   Who are you,
30 that should fret and rage, and bite the chains of Nature?
Nothing worse happens to you than does to all nations who
have extensive empire ; and it happens in all the forms into
which empire can be thrown.   In large bodies the circulation of power must be less vigorous at the extremities.

Nature has said it. The Turk cannot govern Egypt and Arabia and Kurdistan as he governs Thrace; nor has he the same dominion in Crimea and Algiers which he has at Brusa and Smyrna. Despotism itself is obliged to truck and huckster. The sultan gets such obedience as he can. 5 He governs with a loose rein, that he may govern at all; and the whole of the force and vigor of his authority in his centre is derived from a prudent relaxation in all his borders. Spain, in her provinces, is perhaps not so well obeyed as you are in yours. She complies too; she submits; she 10 watches times. This is the immutable condition, the eternal law, of extensive and detached empire.

Then, Sir, from these six capital sources: of descent, of form of government, of religion in the northern provinces, of manners in the southern, of education, of the remoteness 15 of situation from the first mover of government, — from all these causes a fierce spirit of liberty has grown up. It has grown with the growth of the people in your colonies, and increased with the increase of their wealth: a spirit, that unhappily meeting with an exercise of power in England, 20 which, however lawful, is not reconcilable to any ideas of liberty, much less with theirs, has kindled this flame that is ready to consume us.

I do not mean to commend either the spirit in this excess or the moral causes which produce it. Perhaps a more 25 smooth and accommodating spirit of freedom in them would be more acceptable to us. Perhaps ideas of liberty might be desired more reconcilable with an arbitrary and boundless authority. Perhaps we might wish the colonists to be persuaded that their liberty is more secure when held in 30 trust for them by us, as their guardians during a perpetual minority, than with any part of it in their own hands. The question is not whether their spirit deserves praise or blame, but what, in the name of God, shall we do with it? You have before you the object, such as it is, with all its glories, with all its imperfections on its head. You see the magnitude, the importance, the temper, the habits, the disorders. By all these considerations we are strongly urged to determine something concerning it. We are called upon to fix some rule and line for our future conduct, which may give a little stability to our politics and prevent the return of such unhappy deliberations as the present. Every such return will bring the matter before us in a still more untractable form. For what astonishing and incredible things have we not seen already! What monsters have not been generated from this unnatural contention! Whilst every principle of authority and resistance has been pushed, upon both sides, as far as it would go, there is nothing so solid and certain, either in reasoning or in practice, that has not been shaken. Until very lately all authority in America seemed to be nothing but an emanation from yours. Even the popular part of the colony constitution derived all its activity, and its first vital movement, from the pleasure of the crown. We thought, Sir, that the utmost which the discontented colonists could do was to disturb authority; we never dreamt they could of themselves supply it, knowing in general what an operose business it is to establish a government absolutely new. But having for our purposes in this contention resolved that none but an obedient assembly should sit, the humors of the people there, finding all passage through the legal channel stopped, with great violence broke out another way. Some provinces have tried their experiment, as we have tried ours; and theirs has succeeded. They have formed a government sufficient for its purposes, without the bustle of a revolution or the troublesome formality of an election. Evident necessity and tacit consent have done the business in an instant. So well they have done it, that Lord Dunmore (the account is among the fragments on your table) tells you that the new institution is infinitely better obeyed than the ancient government ever was in its most fortunate periods. Obedience is what makes government, and not the names by which it is called : not the name of governor, as formerly ; or committee, as at present. This new government has originated directly from the people, and was not transmitted through any of the ordinary artificial media of a positive constitution. It was not a manufacture ready formed, and transmitted to them in that condition from England. The evil arising from hence is this : that the colonists having once found the possibility of enjoying the advantages of order in the midst of a struggle for liberty, such struggles will not henceforward seem so terrible to the settled and sober part of mankind, as they had appeared before the trial.

Pursuing the same plan of punishing by the denial of the exercise of government to still greater lengths, we wholly abrogated the ancient government of Massachusetts. We were confident that the first feeling, if not the very prospect of anarchy, would instantly enforce a complete submission. The experiment was tried. A new, strange, unexpected face of things appeared. Anarchy is found tolerable. A vast province has now subsisted, and subsisted in a considerable degree of health and vigor, for near a twelvemonth, without governor, without public council, without judges, without executive magistrates. How long it will continue in this state, or what may arise out of this unheard-of situation, how can the wisest of us conjecture ? Our late experience has taught us that many of those fundamental principles formerly believed infallible are either not of the importance they were imagined to be, or that we have not at all adverted to some other far more important and far more powerful principles, which entirely overrule those we had considered as omnipotent. I am much against any further experiments which tend to put to the proof any more of these allowed opinions which contribute so much to the public tranquillity. In effect, we suffer as much at home by this loosening of all ties and this concussion of all established opinions, as we do 5 abroad.   For, in order to prove that the Americans have no right to their liberties, we are every day endeavoring to subvert the maxims which preserve the whole spirit of our own. To prove that Americans ought not to be free, we are obliged to depreciate the value of freedom itself ; and we never seem 10 to gain a paltry advantage over them in debate, without attacking some of those principles, or deriding some of those feelings, for which our ancestors have shed their blood.

But, Sir, in wishing to put an end to pernicious experiments, I do not mean to preclude the fullest inquiry.   Far 15 from it.   Far from deciding on a sudden or partial view, I would patiently go round and round the subject, and survey it minutely in every possible aspect.   Sir, if I were capable of engaging you to an equal attention, I would state that, as far as I am capable of discerning, there are but three ways 20 of proceeding relative to this stubborn spirit which prevails in your colonies and disturbs your government.   These are : to change that spirit as inconvenient, by removing the causes ; to prosecute it as criminal ; or to comply with it as necessary.   I would not be guilty of an imperfect enumeration ; 25 I can think of but these three.   Another has indeed been started, that of giving up the colonies ; but it met so slight a reception that I do not think myself obliged to dwell a great while upon it.   It is nothing but a little sally of anger, like the frowardness of peevish children, who, when they 30 cannot get all they would have, are resolved to take nothing.

The first of these plans, to change the spirit as inconvenient, by removing the causes, I think is the most like a systematic proceeding.   It is radical in its principle ; but it is attended with great difficulties, some of them little short, as

I conceive, of impossibilities. This will appear by examining into the plans which have been proposed.

As the growing population in the colonies is evidently one cause of their resistance, it was last session mentioned in both Houses by men of weight, and received not without applause, that in order to check this evil, it would be proper for the crown to make no further grants of land. But to this scheme there are two objections. The first, that there is already so much unsettled land in private hands as to afford room for an immense future population, although the crown not only withheld its grants, but annihilated its soil. If this be the case, then the only effect of this avarice of desolation, this hoarding of a royal wilderness, would be to raise the value of the possessions in the hands of the great private monopolists, without any adequate check to the growing and alarming mischief of population.

But if you stopped your grants, what would be the consequence? The people would occupy without grants. They have already so occupied in many places. You cannot station garrisons in every part of these deserts. If you drive the people from one place, they will carry on their annual tillage and remove with their flocks and herds to another. Many of the people in the back settlements are already little attached to particular situations. Already they have topped the Appalachian Mountains. From thence they behold before them an immense plain, one vast, rich, level meadow; a square of five hundred miles. Over this they would wander without a possibility of restraint; they would change their manners with the habits of their life; would soon forget a government by which they were disowned; would become hordes of English Tartars, and pouring down upon your unfortified frontiers a fierce and irresistible cavalry, become masters of your governors and your counsellors, your collectors and comptrollers, and of all the slaves that adhered to them. Such would, and in no long time must, be the effect of attempting to forbid as a crime, and to suppress as an evil, the command and blessing of Providence, "Increase and multiply." Such would be the happy result of an endeavor to keep as a lair of wild beasts that earth which God, by an express charter, has given to the children of men. Far different and surely much wiser has been our policy hitherto. Hitherto we have invited our people, by every kind of bounty, to fixed establishments. We have invited the husbandman to look to authority for his title. We have taught him piously to believe in the mysterious virtue of wax and parchment. We have thrown each tract of land, as it was peopled, into districts, that the ruling power should never be wholly out of sight. We have settled all we could; and we have carefully attended every settlement with government.

Adhering, Sir, as I do, to this policy, as well as for the reasons I have just given, I think this new project of hedging-in population to be neither prudent nor practicable.

To impoverish the colonies in general, and in particular to arrest the noble course of their marine enterprises, would be a more easy task. I freely confess it. We have shown a disposition to a system of this kind, — a disposition even to continue the restraint after the offence, looking on ourselves as rivals to our colonies, and persuaded that of course we must gain all that they shall lose. Much mischief we may certainly do. The power inadequate to all other things is often more than sufficient for this. I do not look on the direct and immediate power of the colonies to resist our violence as very formidable. In this, however, I may be mistaken. But when I consider that we have colonies for no purpose but to be serviceable to us, it seems to my poor understanding a little preposterous to make them unserviceable in order to keep them obedient. It is, in truth, nothing more than the old and, as I thought, exploded problem of tyranny, which proposes to beggar its subjects into submission. But remember, when you have completed your system of impoverishment, that Nature still proceeds in her ordinary course ; that discontent will increase with misery ; and that there are critical moments in the fortune of all states, when they who are too weak to contribute to your prosperity may be strong enough to complete your ruin. *Spoliatis arma supersunt.*

The temper and character which prevail in our colonies are, I am afraid, unalterable by any human art. We cannot, I fear, falsify the pedigree of this fierce people and persuade them that they are not sprung from a nation in whose veins the blood of freedom circulates. The language in which they would hear you tell them this tale would detect the imposition ; your speech would betray you. An Englishman is the unfittest person on earth to argue another Englishman into slavery.

I think it is nearly as little in our power to change their republican religion as their free descent, or to substitute the Roman Catholic as a penalty, or the Church of England as an improvement. The mode of inquisition and dragooning is going out of fashion in the Old World ; and I should not confide much to their efficacy in the New. The education of the Americans is also on the same unalterable bottom with their religion. You cannot persuade them to burn their books of curious science ; to banish their lawyers from their courts of laws ; or to quench the lights of their assemblies by refusing to choose those persons who are best read in their privileges. It would be no less impracticable to think of wholly annihilating the popular assemblies in which these lawyers sit. The army, by which we must govern in their place, would be far more chargeable to us ; not quite so effectual ; and perhaps in the end full as difficult to be kept in obedience.

With regard to the high aristocratic spirit of Virginia and the southern colonies, it has been proposed, I know, to reduce it by declaring a general enfranchisement of their slaves. This project has had its advocates and panegyrists; yet I never could argue myself into any opinion of it. Slaves are often much attached to their masters. A general wild offer of liberty would not always be accepted. History furnishes few instances of it. It is sometimes as hard to persuade slaves to be free as it is to compel freemen to be slaves; and in this auspicious scheme we should have both these pleasing tasks on our hands at once. But when we talk of enfranchisement, do we not perceive that the American master may enfranchise too, and arm servile hands in defence of freedom? — a measure to which other people have had recourse more than once, and not without success, in a desperate situation of their affairs.

Slaves as these unfortunate black people are, and dull as all men are from slavery, must they not a little suspect the offer of freedom from that very nation which has sold them to their present masters? from that nation, one of whose causes of quarrel with those masters is their refusal to deal any more in that inhuman traffic? An offer of freedom from England would come rather oddly, shipped to them in an African vessel, which is refused an entry into the ports of Virginia or Carolina, with a cargo of three hundred Angola negroes. It would be curious to see the Guinea captain attempting at the same instant to publish his proclamation of liberty and to advertise his sale of slaves.

But let us suppose all these moral difficulties got over. The ocean remains. You cannot pump this dry; and as long as it continues in its present bed, so long all the causes which weaken authority by distance will continue.

> Ye gods, annihilate but space and time,
> And make two lovers happy!

was a pious and passionate prayer, but just as reasonable as many of the serious wishes of very grave and solemn politicians.

If then, Sir, it seems almost desperate to think of any alterative course for changing the moral causes (and not quite easy to remove the natural) which produce prejudices irreconcilable to the late exercise of our authority, but that the spirit infallibly will continue ; and continuing, will produce such effects as now embarrass us, — the second mode under consideration is to prosecute that spirit in its overt acts as *criminal.*

At this proposition I must pause a moment. The thing seems a great deal too big for my ideas of jurisprudence. It should seem to my way of conceiving such matters, that there is a very wide difference in reason and policy between the mode of proceeding on the irregular conduct of scattered individuals, or even of bands of men, who disturb order within the state, and the civil dissensions which may, from time to time, on great questions, agitate the several communities which compose a great empire. It looks to me to be narrow and pedantic to apply the ordinary ideas of criminal justice to this great public contest. [I do not know the method of drawing up an indictment against a whole people.] I cannot insult and ridicule the feelings of millions of my fellow-creatures, as Sir Edward Coke insulted one excellent individual (Sir Walter Ralegh) at the bar. I am not ripe to pass sentence on the gravest public bodies, entrusted with magistracies of great authority and dignity, and charged with the safety of their fellow-citizens, upon the very same title that I am. I really think that for wise men this is not judicious ; for sober men, not decent ; for minds tinctured with humanity, not mild and merciful.

Perhaps, Sir, I am mistaken in my idea of an empire as distinguished from a single state or kingdom. But my idea

of it is this : (that an empire is the aggregate of many states
under one common head, whether this head be a monarch
or a presiding republic.) It does in such constitutions frequently happen (and nothing but the dismal, cold, dead uni-
5 formity of servitude can prevent its happening) that the subordinate parts have many local privileges and immunities.
Between these privileges and the supreme common authority
the line may be extremely nice.   Of course disputes — often,
too, very bitter disputes — and much ill blood will arise.   But
10 though every privilege is an exemption (in the case) from
the ordinary exercise of the supreme authority, it is no denial
of it.   The claim of a privilege seems rather, *ex vi termini,*
to imply a superior power ; for to talk of the privileges of a
state, or of a person who has no superior, is hardly any
15 better than speaking nonsense.   Now in such unfortunate
quarrels among the component parts of a great political
union of communities, I can scarcely conceive anything
more completely imprudent than for the head of the empire
to insist that, if any privilege is pleaded against his will or
20 his acts, [that] his whole authority is denied ; instantly to pro-
claim rebellion, to beat to arms, and to put the offending provinces under the ban.   Will not this, Sir, very soon teach the
provinces to make no distinctions on their part ?   Will it
not teach them that the government against which a claim
25 of liberty is tantamount to high treason is a government to
which submission is equivalent to slavery ?   It may not
always be quite convenient to impress dependent communities with such an idea.

We are, indeed, in all disputes with the colonies, by the
30 necessity of things, the judge.   It is true, Sir.   But I confess
that the character of judge in my own cause is a thing that
frightens me.   Instead of filling me with pride, I am exceedingly humbled by it.   I cannot proceed with a stern, assured,
judicial confidence, until I find myself in something more

like a judicial character. I must have these hesitations as long as I am compelled to recollect that, in my little reading upon such contests as these, the sense of mankind has at least as often decided against the superior as the subordinate power. Sir, let me add, too, that the opinion of my having some abstract right in my favor would not put me much at my ease in passing sentence, unless I could be sure that there were no rights which, in their exercise under certain circumstances, were not the most odious of all wrongs and the most vexatious of all injustice. Sir, these considerations have great weight with me, when I find things so circumstanced, that I see the same party at once a civil litigant against me in point of right and a culprit before me, while I sit as a criminal judge on acts of his, whose moral quality is to be decided upon the merits of that very litigation. Men are every now and then put, by the complexity of human affairs, into strange situations; but justice is the same, let the judge be in what situation he will.

There is, Sir, also a circumstance which convinces me that this mode of criminal proceeding is not (at least in the present stage of our contest) altogether expedient, which is nothing less than the conduct of those very persons who have seemed to adopt that mode, by lately declaring a rebellion in Massachusetts Bay, as they had formerly addressed to have traitors brought hither, under an act of Henry the Eighth, for trial. For though rebellion is declared, it is not proceeded against as such; nor have any steps been taken towards the apprehension or conviction of any individual offender, either on our late or our former address; but modes of public coercion have been adopted, and such as have much more resemblance to a sort of qualified hostility towards an independent power than the punishment of rebellious subjects. All this seems rather inconsistent; but it shows how difficult it is to apply these juridical ideas to our present case.

In this situation, let us seriously and cooly ponder. What is it we have got by all our menaces, which have been many and ferocious? What advantage have we derived from the penal laws we have passed, and which, for the time, have 5 been severe and numerous? What advances have we made towards our object, by the sending of a force which, by land and sea, is no contemptible strength? Has the disorder abated? Nothing less. When I see things in this situation, after such confident hopes, bold promises and active 10 exertions, I cannot for my life avoid a suspicion that the plan itself is not correctly right.

If, then, the removal of the causes of this spirit of American liberty be for the greater part, or rather entirely, impracticable ; if the ideas of criminal process be inapplicable, or, 15 if applicable, are in the highest degree inexpedient; what way yet remains? No way is open but the third and last, — to comply with the American spirit as necessary ; or, if you please, to submit to it as a necessary evil.

If we adopt this mode, if we mean to conciliate and con-
20 cede, let us see of what nature the concession ought to be. To ascertain the nature of our concession, we must look at their complaint. The colonies complain that they have not the characteristic mark and seal of British freedom. They complain that they are taxed in a Parliament in which they 25 are not represented. If you mean to satisfy them at all, you must satisfy them with regard to this complaint. If you mean to please any people, you must give them the boon which they ask, — not what you may think better for them, but of a kind totally different. Such an act may be 30 a wise regulation, but it is no concession ; whereas our present theme is the mode of giving satisfaction.

Sir, I think you must perceive that I am resolved this day to have nothing at all to do with the question of the right of taxation. Some gentlemen startle, — but it is true ;

refutation

I put it totally out of the question. It is less than nothing in my consideration. I do not indeed wonder, nor will you, Sir, that gentlemen of profound learning are fond of displaying it on this profound subject. But my consideration is narrow, confined, and wholly limited to the policy of the question. I do not examine whether the giving away a man's money be a power excepted and reserved out of the general trust of government ; and how far all mankind, in all forms of polity, are entitled to an exercise of that right by the charter of Nature ; or whether, on the contrary, a right of taxation is necessarily involved in the general principle of legislation and inseparable from the ordinary supreme power. These are deep questions, where great names militate against each other ; where reason is perplexed ; and an appeal to authorities only thickens the confusion : for high and reverend authorities lift up their heads on both sides ; and there is no sure footing in the middle. This point is the great

> Serbonian bog,
> Betwixt Damiata and Mount Casius old,
> Where armies whole have sunk.

I do not intend to be overwhelmed in that bog, though in such respectable company. The question with me is not whether you have a right to render your people miserable, but whether it is not your interest to make them happy. It is not what a lawyer tells me I *may* do, but what humanity, reason and justice tell me I *ought* to do. Is a politic act the worse for being a generous one ? Is no concession proper but that which is made from your want of right to keep what you grant ? Or does it lessen the grace or dignity of relaxing in the exercise of an odious claim, because you have your evidence-room full of titles and your magazines stuffed with arms to enforce them ? What signify all those titles and all those arms ? Of what avail are they, when the reason of the thing tells me that the assertion of my title is the loss of my suit; and that I could do nothing but wound myself by the use of my own weapons?

Such is steadfastly my opinion of the absolute necessity of keeping up the concord of this empire by a unity of spirit, though in a diversity of operations, that if I were sure the colonists had at their leaving this country sealed a regular compact of servitude, that they had solemnly abjured all the rights of citizens, that they had made a vow to renounce all ideas of liberty for them and their posterity to all generations; yet I should hold myself obliged to conform to the temper I found universally prevalent in my own day, and to govern two million of men, impatient of servitude, on the principles of freedom. I am not determining a point of law; I am restoring tranquillity: and the general character and situation of a people must determine what sort of government is fitted for them. That point nothing else can or ought to determine.

My idea, therefore, without considering whether we yield as matter of right or grant as matter of favor, is *to admit the people of our colonies into an interest in the Constitution,* and by recording that admission in the journals of Parliament, to give them as strong an assurance as the nature of the thing will admit, that we mean forever to adhere to that solemn declaration of systematic indulgence.

Some years ago, the repeal of a revenue act, upon its understood principle, might have served to show that we intended an unconditional abatement of the exercise of a taxing power. Such a measure was then sufficient to remove all suspicion and to give perfect content. But unfortunate events since that time may make something further necessary; and not more necessary for the satisfaction of the colonies than for the dignity and consistency of our own future proceedings.

I have taken a very incorrect measure of the disposition of the House, if this proposal in itself would be received with dislike. I think, Sir, we have few American financiers. But our misfortune is, we are too acute; we are too exquisite in our conjectures of the future, for men oppressed with such great and present evils. The more moderate among the opposers of parliamentary concession freely confess that they hope no good from taxation; but they apprehend the colonists have further views, and if this point were conceded, they would instantly attack the trade laws. These gentlemen are convinced that this was the intention from the beginning, and the quarrel of the Americans with taxation was no more than a cloak and cover to this design. Such has been the language, even of a gentleman of real moderation and of a natural temper well adjusted to fair and equal government. I am, however, Sir, not a little surprised at this kind of discourse whenever I hear it; and I am the more surprised on account of the arguments which I constantly find in company with it, and which are often urged from the same mouths and on the same day.

For instance, when we allege that it is against reason to tax a people under so many restraints in trade as the Americans, the noble lord in the blue ribbon shall tell you that the restraints on trade are futile and useless, of no advantage to us, and of no burden to those on whom they are imposed; that the trade to America is not secured by the Acts of Navigation, but by the natural and irresistible advantage of a commercial preference.

Such is the merit of the trade laws in this posture of the debate. But when strong internal circumstances are urged against the taxes; when the scheme is dissected; when experience and the nature of things are brought to prove, and do prove, the utter impossibility of obtaining an effective revenue from the colonies; — when these things are pressed,

or rather press themselves, so as to drive the advocates of
colony taxes to a clear admission of the futility of the scheme;
then, Sir, the sleeping trade laws revive from their trance,
and this useless taxation is to be kept sacred, not for its own
5 sake, but as a counterguard and security of the laws of
trade.

Then, Sir, you keep up revenue laws which are mischievous, in order to preserve trade laws that are useless.   Such
is the wisdom of our plan in both its members.   They are
10 separately given up as of no value; and yet one is always to
be defended for the sake of the other.   But I cannot agree
with the noble lord nor with the pamphlet from whence he
seems to have borrowed these ideas concerning the inutility
of the trade laws; for without idolizing them, I am sure they
15 are still in many ways of great use to us, and in former
times they have been of the greatest.   They do confine, and
they do greatly narrow, the market for the Americans.   But
my perfect conviction of this does not help me in the least
to discern how the revenue laws form any security what-
20 soever to the commercial regulations; or that these commercial regulations are the true ground of the quarrel; or that
the giving way in any one instance of authority is to lose all
that may remain unconceded.

One fact is clear and indisputable: the public and avowed
25 origin of this quarrel was on taxation.   This quarrel has
indeed brought on new disputes on new questions; but
certainly the least bitter and the fewest of all on the trade
laws.   To judge which of the two be the real, radical cause
of quarrel, we have to see whether the commercial dispute
30 did, in order of time, precede the dispute on taxation?
There is not a shadow of evidence for it.   Next, to enable
us to judge whether at this moment a dislike to the trade
laws be the real cause of quarrel, it is absolutely necessary
to put the taxes out of the question by a repeal.   See how

the Americans act in this position, and then you will be able to discern correctly what is the true object of the controversy, or whether any controversy at all will remain. Unless you consent to remove this cause of difference, it is impossible with decency to assert that the dispute is not upon what it is avowed to be. And I would, Sir, recommend to your serious consideration, whether it be prudent to form a rule for punishing people, not on their own acts, but on your conjectures. Surely it is preposterous at the very best. It is not justifying your anger by their misconduct, but it is converting your ill-will into their delinquency.

75 But the colonies will go further. Alas! alas! when will this speculating against fact and reason end? What will quiet these panic fears which we entertain of the hostile effect of a conciliatory conduct? Is it true that no case can exist in which it is proper for the sovereign to accede to the desires of his discontented subjects? Is there anything peculiar in this case to make a rule for itself? Is all authority of course lost, when it is not pushed to the extreme? Is it a certain maxim that the fewer causes of dissatisfaction are left by government, the more the subject will be inclined to resist and rebel?

76 All these objections being in fact no more than suspicions, conjectures, divinations, formed in defiance of fact and experience, they did not, Sir, discourage me from entertaining the idea of a conciliatory concession, founded on the principles which I have just stated.

77 In forming a plan for this purpose, I endeavored to put myself in that frame of mind which was the most natural and the most reasonable, and which was certainly the most probable means of securing me from all error. I set out with a perfect distrust of my own abilities, a total renunciation of every speculation of my own: and with a profound reverence for the wisdom of our ancestors, who have left us

the inheritance of so happy a constitution and so flourishing an empire, and, what is a thousand times more valuable, the treasury of the maxims and principles which formed the one and obtained the other.

5 During the reigns of the kings of Spain of the Austrian family, whenever they were at a loss in the Spanish councils, it was common for their statesmen to say that they ought to consult the genius of Philip the Second. The genius of Philip the Second might mislead them; and the issue of 10 their affairs showed that they had not chosen the most perfect standard. But, Sir, I am sure that I shall not be misled, when in a case of constitutional difficulty I consult the genius of the English Constitution. Consulting at that oracle (it was with all due humility and piety), I found four 15 capital examples in a similar case before me: those of Ireland, Wales, Chester and Durham.

Ireland before the English conquest, though never governed by a despotic power, had no Parliament. How far the English Parliament itself was at that time modelled 20 according to the present form is disputed among antiquarians. But we have all the reason in the world to be assured that a form of Parliament such as England then enjoyed she instantly communicated to Ireland; and we are equally sure that almost every successive improvement in constitutional 25 liberty, as fast as it was made here, was transmitted thither. The feudal baronage and the feudal knighthood, the roots of our primitive constitution, were early transplanted into that soil, and grew and flourished there. Magna Charta, if it did not give us originally the House of Commons, gave us 30 at least an House of Commons of weight and consequence. But your ancestors did not churlishly sit down alone to the feast of Magna Charta. Ireland was made immediately a partaker. This benefit of English laws and liberties, I confess, was not at first extended to *all* Ireland. Mark the consequence. English authority and English liberties had exactly the same boundaries. Your standard could never be advanced an inch before your privileges. Sir John Davies shows beyond a doubt that the refusal of a general communication of these rights was the true cause why Ireland was five hundred years in subduing; and after the vain projects of a military government, attempted in the reign of Queen Elizabeth, it was soon discovered that nothing could make that country English in civility and allegiance, but your laws and your forms of legislature. It was not English arms, but the English Constitution, that conquered Ireland. From that time Ireland has ever had a general Parliament, as she had before a partial Parliament. You changed the people, you altered the religion, but you never touched the form or the vital substance of free government in that kingdom. You deposed kings; you restored them; you altered the succession to theirs as well as to your own crown; but you never altered their constitution, the principle of which was respected by usurpation, restored with the restoration of monarchy, and established, I trust, forever by the glorious Revolution. This has made Ireland the great and flourishing kingdom that it is; and from a disgrace and a burden intolerable to this nation, has rendered her a principal part of our strength and ornament. This country cannot be said to have ever formally taxed her. The irregular things done in the confusion of mighty troubles and on the hinge of great revolutions, even if all were done that is said to have been done, form no example. If they have any effect in argument, they make an exception to prove the rule. None of your own liberties could stand a moment, if the casual deviations from them at such times were suffered to be used as proofs of their nullity. By the lucrative amount of such casual breaches in the Constitution, judge what the stated and fixed rule of supply has been in that kingdom.

Your Irish pensioners would starve, if they had no other
fund to live on than taxes granted by English authority.
Turn your eyes to those popular grants from whence all your
great supplies are come, and learn to respect that only
5 source of public wealth in the British Empire.

My next example is Wales. This country was said to be
reduced by Henry the Third. It was said more truly to be
so by Edward the First. But though then conquered, it was
not looked upon as any part of the realm of England. Its
10 old constitution, whatever that might have been, was
destroyed, and no good one was substituted in its place.
The care of that tract was put into the hands of Lords
Marchers, — a form of government of a very singular kind,
a strange, heterogeneous monster, something between hos-
15 tility and government; perhaps it has a sort of resemblance,
according to the modes of those times, to that of commander-
in-chief at present, to whom all civil power is granted as
secondary. The manners of the Welsh nation followed the
genius of the government : the people were ferocious, restive,
20 savage and uncultivated, sometimes composed, never paci-
fied. Wales, within itself, was in perpetual disorder ; and
it kept the frontier of England in perpetual alarm. Benefits
from it to the state there were none. Wales was only known
to England by incursion and invasion.

25 Sir, during that state of things Parliament was not idle.
They attempted to subdue the fierce spirit of the Welsh by
all sorts of rigorous laws. They prohibited by statute the
sending all sorts of arms into Wales, as you prohibit by
proclamation (with something more of doubt on the legality)
30 the sending arms to America. They disarmed the Welsh
by statute, as you attempted (but still with more question
on the legality) to disarm New England by an instruction.
They made an act to drag offenders from Wales into England for trial, as you have done (but with more hardship)

with regard to America. By another act, where one of the parties was an Englishman, they ordained that his trial should be always by English. They made acts to restrain trade, as you do; and they prevented the Welsh from the use of fairs and markets, as you do the Americans from fisheries and foreign ports. In short, when the statute-book was not quite so much swelled as it is now, you find no less than fifteen acts of penal regulation on the subject of Wales.

Here we rub our hands — A fine body of precedents for the authority of Parliament and the use of it! — I admit it fully; and pray add likewise to these precedents, that all the while Wales rid this kingdom like an *incubus;* that it was an unprofitable and oppressive burden; and that an Englishman travelling in that country could not go six yards from the highroad without being murdered.

The march of the human mind is slow. Sir, it was not until after two hundred years discovered that by an eternal law Providence had decreed vexation to violence, and poverty to rapine. Your ancestors did, however, at length open their eyes to the ill-husbandry of injustice. They found that the tyranny of a free people could of all tyrannies the least be endured; and that laws made against an whole nation were not the most effectual methods for securing its obedience. Accordingly, in the twenty-seventh year of Henry the Eighth, the course was entirely altered. With a preamble stating the entire and perfect rights of the crown of England, it gave to the Welsh all the rights and privileges of English subjects. A political order was established; the military power gave way to the civil; the marches were turned into counties. But that a nation should have a right to English liberties, and yet no share at all in the fundamental security of these liberties, — the grant of their own property, — seemed a thing so incongruous that eight years

after, — that is, in the thirty-fifth of that reign, — a complete and not ill-proportioned representation by counties and boroughs was bestowed upon Wales by act of Parliament.   From that moment, as by a charm, the tumults sub-
5 sided; obedience was restored; peace, order and civilization followed in the train of liberty.   When the day-star of the English Constitution had arisen in their hearts, all was harmony within and without: —

— Simul alba nautis
10   Stella refulsit,
Defluit saxis agitatus humor ;
Concidunt venti, fugiuntque nubes,
Et minax (quod sic voluere) ponto
Unda recumbit.

15   The very same year the County Palatine of Chester received the same relief from its oppressions and the same remedy to its disorders.   Before this time Chester was little less distempered than Wales.   The inhabitants, without rights themselves, were the fittest to destroy the rights of
20 others; and from thence Richard the Second drew the standing army of archers with which for a time he oppressed England.   The people of Chester applied to Parliament in a petition penned as I shall read to you: —

To the King our Sovereign Lord, in most humble wise shewen
25 unto your most excellent Majesty the inhabitants of your Grace's County Palatine of Chester : (1) That where the said County Palatine of Chester is and hath been always hitherto exempt, excluded and separated out and from your high court of Parliament, to have any knights and burgesses within the said court ; by reason
30 whereof the said inhabitants have hitherto sustained manifold disherisons, losses and damages, as well in their lands, goods and bodies, as in the good, civil and politic governance and maintenance of the commonwealth of their said country.   (2) And forasmuch as the said inhabitants have always hitherto been

bound by the acts and statutes made and ordained by your said
Highness and your most noble progenitors, by authority of the
said court, as far forth as other counties, cities and boroughs
have been, that have had their knights and burgesses within your
said court of Parliament, and yet have had neither knight ne   5
burgess there for the said County Palatine; the said inhabitants,
for lack thereof, have been oftentimes touched and grieved with
acts and statutes made within the said court, as well derogatory
unto the most ancient jurisdictions, liberties and privileges of
your said County Palatine, as prejudicial unto the commonwealth, 10
quietness, rest and peace of your Grace's most bounden subjects
inhabiting within the same.

What did Parliament with this audacious address? Reject it as a libel? Treat it as an affront to government?
Spurn it as a derogation from the rights of legislature?   15
Did they toss it over the table? Did they burn it by the
hands of the common hangman? They took the petition
of grievance, all rugged as it was, without softening or
temperament, unpurged of the original bitterness and in-
dignation of complaint; they made it the very preamble to   20
their act of redress, and consecrated its principle to all
ages in the sanctuary of legislation.

Here is my third example. It was attended with the
success of the two former. Chester, civilized as well as
Wales, has demonstrated that freedom, and not servitude,   25
is the cure for anarchy; as religion, and not atheism, is the
true remedy for superstition. Sir, this pattern of Chester
was followed in the reign of Charles the Second with regard
to the County Palatine of Durham, which is my fourth
example. This county had long lain out of the pale of   30
free legislation. So scrupulously was the example of Chester followed, that the style of the preamble is nearly the
same with that of the Chester act; and without affecting
the abstract extent of the authority of Parliament, it recog-

James Barrington appointed justice of the *counties in Wales. Born 1727*

48   *SPEECH ON CONCILIATION WITH AMERICA.*

nizes the equity of not suffering any considerable district in which the British subjects may act as a body, to be taxed without their own voice in the grant.

Now if the doctrines of policy contained in these pre-
5 ambles and the force of these examples in the acts of Parliaments avail anything, what can be said against apply-ing them with regard to America? Are not the people of America as much Englishmen as the Welsh? The preamble of the act of Henry the Eighth says the Welsh speak a
10 language no way resembling that of his Majesty's English subjects. Are the Americans not as numerous? If we may trust the learned and accurate Judge Barrington's account of North Wales, and take that as a standard to measure the rest, there is no comparison. The people
15 cannot amount to above 200,000, — not a tenth part of the number in the colonies. Is America in rebellion? Wales was hardly ever free from it. Have you attempted to gov-ern America by penal statutes? You made fifteen for Wales. But your legislative authority is perfect with re-
20 gard to America. Was it less perfect in Wales, Chester, and Durham? But America is virtually represented. What! does the electric force of virtual representation more easily pass over the Atlantic than pervade Wales, which lies in your neighborhood? or than Chester and
25 Durham, surrounded by abundance of representation that is actual and palpable? But, Sir, your ancestors thought this sort of virtual representation, however ample, to be totally insufficient for the freedom of the inhabitants of territories that are so near and comparatively so inconsid-
30 erable. How then can I think it sufficient for those which are infinitely greater and infinitely more remote?

You will now, Sir, perhaps imagine that I am on the point of proposing to you a scheme for a representation of the colonies in Parliament. Perhaps I might be inclined to

entertain some such thought; but a great flood stops me in my course. *Opposuit natura* — I cannot remove the eternal barriers of the creation. The thing, in that mode, I do not know to be possible. As I meddle with no theory, I do not absolutely assert the impracticability of such a represen- 5
tation : but I do not see my way to it; and those who have been more confident have not been more successful. How-ever, the arm of public benevolence is not shortened, and there are often several means to the same end. What Nature has disjoined in one way Wisdom may unite in 10
another. When we cannot give the benefit as we would wish, let us not refuse it altogether. If we cannot give the principal, let us find a substitute. But how? Where? What substitute?

Fortunately I am not obliged for the ways and means of 15
this substitute to tax my own unproductive invention. I am not even obliged to go to the rich treasury of the fertile framers of imaginary commonwealths, not to the *Republic* of Plato, not to the *Utopia* of More, not to the *Oceana* of Harrington. It is before me; it is at my feet, — 20

               And the rude swain
        Treads daily on it with his clouted shoon.

I only wish you to recognize, for the theory, the ancient constitutional policy of this kingdom with regard to repre-sentation, as that policy has been declared in acts of Parlia- 25
ment; and as to the practice, to return to that mode which an uniform experience has marked out to you as best, and in which you walked with security, advantage and honor, until the year 1763.

My resolutions therefore mean to establish the equity and 30
justice of a taxation of America by *grant,* and not by *impo-sition;* to mark the *legal competency* of the colony assemblies for the support of their government in peace and for public

aids in time of war; to acknowledge that this legal competency has had *a dutiful and beneficial exercise;* and that experience has shown the *benefit of their grants* and the *futility of parliamentary taxation as a method of supply.*

These solid truths compose six fundamental propositions. There are three more resolutions corollary to these. If you admit the first set, you can hardly reject the others. But if you admit the first, I shall be far from solicitous whether you accept or refuse the last. I think these six massive pillars will be of strength sufficient to support the temple of British concord. I have no more doubt than I entertain of my existence that, if you admitted these, you would command an immediate peace and, with but tolerable future management, a lasting obedience in America. I am not arrogant in this confident assurance. The propositions are all mere matters of fact; and if they are such facts as draw irresistible conclusions even in the stating, this is the power of truth, and not any management of mine.

Sir, I shall open the whole plan to you together, with such observations on the motions as may tend to illustrate them where they may want explanation. The first is a resolution, —

That the colonies and plantations of Great Britain in North America, consisting of fourteen separate governments, and containing two millions and upwards of free inhabitants, have not had the liberty and privilege of electing and sending any knights and burgesses, or others, to represent them in the high court of Parliament.

This is a plain matter of fact, necessary to be laid down, and (excepting the description) it is laid down in the language of the constitution; it is taken nearly *verbatim* from acts of Parliament.

The second is like unto the first, —

That the said colonies and plantations have been liable to, and bounden by, several subsidies, payments, rates and taxes, given and granted by Parliament, though the said colonies and plantations have not their knights and burgesses in the said high court of Parliament, of their own election, to represent the condition of their country; by lack whereof they have been oftentimes touched and grieved by subsidies given, granted and assented to, in the said court, in a manner prejudicial to the commonwealth, quietness, rest and peace of the subjects inhabiting within the same.

Is this description too hot or too cold, too strong or too weak? Does it arrogate too much to the supreme legislature? Does it lean too much to the claims of the people? If it runs into any of these errors, the fault is not mine. It is the language of your own ancient acts of Parliament:—

> Non meus hic sermo, sed quae praecepit Ofellus,
> Rusticus, abnormis sapiens.

It is the genuine produce of the ancient, rustic, manly, home-bred sense of this country,—I did not dare to rub off a particle of the venerable rust that rather adorns and preserves, than destroys, the metal. It would be a profanation to touch with a tool the stones which construct the sacred altar of peace. I would not violate with modern polish the ingenuous and noble roughness of these truly constitutional materials. Above all things, I was resolved not to be guilty of tampering,—the odious vice of restless and unstable minds. I put my foot in the tracks of our forefathers, where I can neither wander nor stumble. Determining to fix articles of peace, I was resolved not to be wise beyond what was written; I was resolved to use nothing else than the form of sound words, to let others abound in their own sense, and carefully to abstain from all expressions of my own. What the law has said, I say. In all things else I am silent. I have no organ but for her words. This, if it be not ingenious, I am sure is safe.

There are indeed words expressive of grievance in this second resolution, which those who are resolved always to
5 be in the right will deny to contain matter of fact, as applied to the present case, although Parliament thought them true with regard to the counties of Chester and Durham. They will deny that the Americans were ever "touched and grieved" with the taxes. If they consider nothing in taxes
10 but their weight as pecuniary impositions, there might be some pretence for this denial. But men may be sorely touched and deeply grieved in their privileges as well as in their purses. Men may lose little in property by the act which takes away all their freedom. When a man is robbed
15 of a trifle on the highway, it is not the twopence lost that constitutes the capital outrage. This is not confined to privileges. Even ancient indulgences withdrawn, without offence on the part of those who enjoyed such favors, operate as grievances. But were the Americans then not
20 touched and grieved by the taxes, in some measure, merely as taxes? If so, why were they almost all either wholly repealed or exceedingly reduced? Were they not touched and grieved even by the regulating duties of the sixth of George the Second? Else why were the duties first reduced
25 to one-third in 1764, and afterwards to a third of that third in the year 1766? Were they not touched and grieved by the Stamp Act? I shall say they were, until that tax is revived. Were they not touched and grieved by the duties of 1767, which were likewise repealed, and which Lord
30 Hillsborough tells you (for the ministry) were laid contrary to the true principle of commerce? Is not the assurance given by that noble person to the colonies of a resolution to lay no more taxes on them, an admission that taxes would touch and grieve them? Is not the resolution of the noble

lord in the blue ribbon, now standing on your journals, the strongest of all proofs that parliamentary subsidies really touched and grieved them? Else why all these changes, modifications, repeals, assurances and resolutions?

The next proposition is, —   5

5 That, from the distance of the said colonies and from other circumstances, no method hath hitherto been devised for procuring a representation in Parliament for the said colonies.

This is an assertion of a fact. I go no further on the paper; though in my private judgment a useful representa- 10 tion is impossible. I am sure it is not desired by them; nor ought it, perhaps, by us: but I abstain from opinions.

The fourth resolution is, —

That each of the said colonies hath within itself a body, chosen in part or in the whole by the freemen, freeholders or other free 15 inhabitants thereof, commonly called the general assembly, or general court; with powers legally to raise, levy and assess, according to the several usage of such colonies, duties and taxes towards defraying all sorts of public services.

This competence in the colony assemblies is certain. It 20 is proved by the whole tenor of their acts of supply in all the assemblies, in which the constant style of granting is, "An aid to his Majesty"; and acts granting to the crown have regularly for near a century passed the public offices without dispute. Those who have been pleased paradoxically to 25 deny this right, holding that none but the British Parliament can grant to the crown, are wished to look to what is done, not only in the colonies, but in Ireland, in one uniform, unbroken tenor every session. Sir, I am surprised that this doctrine should come from some of the law servants of the 30 crown. I say that if the crown could be responsible, his Majesty — but certainly the ministers, and even these law officers themselves through whose hands the acts pass,

biennially in Ireland or annually in the colonies, are in an
habitual course of committing impeachable offences.   What
habitual offenders have been all presidents of the council, all
secretaries of state, all first lords of trade, all attorneys and
all solicitors-general !   However, they are safe, as no one
impeaches them ; and there is no ground of charge against
them, except in their own unfounded theories.

The fifth resolution is also a resolution of fact, —

That the said general assemblies, general courts, or other
bodies legally qualified as aforesaid, have at sundry times freely
granted several large subsidies and public aids for his Majesty's
service, according to their abilities, when required thereto by letter
from one of his Majesty's principal secretaries of state; and that
their right to grant the same and their cheerfulness and sufficiency
in the said grants have been at sundry times acknowledged by
Parliament

To say nothing of their great expenses in the Indian wars,
and not to take their exertion in foreign ones so high as the
supplies in the year 1695, not to go back to their public
contributions in the year 1710, I shall begin to travel only
where the journals give me light, — resolving to deal in
nothing but fact authenticated by parliamentary record, and
to build myself wholly on that solid basis.

On the 4th of April, 1748, a committee of this House came
to the following resolution: —

Resolved, That it is the opinion of this committee *that it is just
and reasonable* that the several provinces and colonies of Massachusetts Bay, New Hampshire, Connecticut and Rhode Island,
be reimbursed the expenses they have been at in taking and
securing to the crown of Great Britain the island of Cape Breton
and its dependencies.

These expenses were immense for such colonies.   They
were above £200,000 sterling: money first raised and advanced on their public credit.

On the 28th of January, 1756, a message from the king came to us to this effect : —

His Majesty, being sensible of the zeal and vigor with which his faithful subjects of certain colonies in North America have exerted themselves in defence of his Majesty's just rights and possessions, recommends it to this House to take the same into their consideration, and to enable his Majesty to give them such assistance as may be a *proper reward and encouragement.*

On the 3d of February, 1756, the House came to a suitable resolution, expressed in words nearly the same as those of the message; but with the further addition that the money then voted was as an *encouragement* to the colonies to exert themselves with vigor.   It will not be necessary to go through all the testimonies which your own records have given to the truth of my resolutions.   I will only refer you to the places in the journals: —

Vol. XXVII. — 16th and 19th May, 1757.

Vol. XXVIII. — June 1st, 1758 ; April 26th and 30th, 1759 ; March 26th and 31st, and April 28th, 1760; Jan. 9th and 20th, 1761.

Vol. XXIX. — Jan. 22nd and 26th, 1762 ; March 14th and 17th, 1763.

Sir, here is the repeated acknowledgment of Parliament that the colonies not only gave, but gave to satiety.   This nation has formally acknowledged two things : first, that the colonies had gone beyond their abilities, Parliament having thought it necessary to reimburse them ; secondly, that they had acted legally and laudably in their grants of money and their maintenance of troops, since the compensation is expressly given as reward and encouragement.   Reward is not bestowed for acts that are unlawful ; and encouragement is not held out to things that deserve reprehension. My resolution therefore does nothing more than collect into one proposition what is scattered through your journals.   I

give you nothing but your own; and you cannot refuse in the gross what you have so often acknowledged in detail. The admission of this, which will be so honorable to them and to you, will indeed be mortal to all the miserable stories
5 by which the passions of the misguided people have been engaged in an unhappy system. The people heard, indeed, from the beginning of these disputes, one thing continually dinned in their ears, — that reason and justice demanded that the Americans, who paid no taxes, should be compelled
10 to contribute. How did that fact of their paying nothing stand when the taxing system began? When Mr. Grenville began to form his system of American revenue, he stated in this House that the colonies were then in debt two millions six hundred thousand pounds sterling money, and
15 was of opinion they would discharge that debt in four years. On this state, those untaxed people were actually subject to the payment of taxes to the amount of six hundred and fifty thousand a year. In fact, however, Mr. Grenville was mistaken. The funds given for sinking the debt did not prove
20 quite so ample as both the colonies and he expected. The calculation was too sanguine: the reduction was not completed till some years after, and at different times in different colonies. However, the taxes after the war continued too great to bear any addition with prudence or propriety; and
25 when the burdens imposed in consequence of former requisitions were discharged, our tone became too high to resort again to requisition. No colony since that time ever has had any requisition whatsoever made to it.

We see the sense of the crown and the sense of Parliament
30 on the productive nature of a *revenue by grant*. Now search the same journals for the produce of the *revenue by imposition*. Where is it? Let us know the volume and the page. What is the gross, what is the net produce? To what service is it applied? How have you appropriated its surplus?

What, can none of the many skilful index-makers that we are now employing find any trace of it? Well, let them and that rest together. But are the journals, which say nothing of the revenue, as silent on the discontent? Oh, no! a child may find it. It is the melancholy burden and 5 blot of every page.

I think, then, I am, from those journals, justified in the sixth and last resolution, which is, —

That it hath been found by experience that the manner of granting the said supplies and aids by the said general assemblies 10 hath been more agreeable to the said colonies, and more beneficial and conducive to the public service, than the mode of giving and granting aids in Parliament, to be raised and paid in the said colonies.

This makes the whole of the fundamental part of the plan. 15 The conclusion is irresistible. You cannot say that you were driven by any necessity to an exercise of the utmost rights of legislature. You cannot assert that you took on yourselves the task of imposing colony taxes, from the want of another legal body that is competent to the purpose of 20 supplying the exigencies of the state without wounding the prejudices of the people. Neither is it true that the body so qualified and having that competence had neglected the duty.

The question now, on all this accumulated matter, is, — whether you will choose to abide by a profitable experience 25 or a mischievous theory; whether you choose to build on imagination or fact; whether you prefer enjoyment or hope; satisfaction in your subjects or discontent?

If these propositions are accepted, everything which has been made to enforce a contrary system must, I take it for 30 granted, fall along with it. On that ground I have drawn the following resolution, which, when it comes to be moved, will naturally be divided in a proper manner: —

That it may be proper to repeal an act made in the seventh year of the reign of his present Majesty, entitled, " An act for granting certain duties in the British colonies and plantations in America ; for allowing a drawback of the duties of customs upon 5 the exportation from this kingdom, of coffee and cocoanuts of the produce of the said colonies or plantations ; for discontinuing the drawbacks payable on China earthenware exported to America ; and for more effectually preventing the clandestine running of goods in the said colonies and plantations."— And that it may be 10 proper to repeal an act made in the fourteenth year of the reign of his present Majesty, entitled, " An act to discontinue, in such manner and for such time as are therein mentioned, the landing and discharging, lading or shipping, of goods, wares and merchandise, at the town and within the harbor of Boston, in the province 15 of Massachusetts Bay, in North America."— And that it may be proper to repeal an act made in the fourteenth year of the reign of his present Majesty, entitled, " An act for the impartial administration of justice in the cases of persons questioned for any acts done by them in the execution of the law, or for the suppression 20 of riots and tumults, in the province of Massachusetts Bay, in New England."— And that it may be proper to repeal an act made in the fourteenth year of the reign of his present Majesty, entitled, " An act for the better regulating the government of the province of the Massachusetts Bay, in New England."— And also, that it 25 may be proper to explain and amend an act made in the thirty-fifth year of the reign of King Henry the Eighth, entitled, " An act for the trial of treasons committed out of the king's dominions."

I wish, Sir, to repeal the Boston Port Bill, because (independently of the dangerous precedent of suspending the 30 rights of the subject during the king's pleasure) it was passed, as I apprehend, with less regularity and on more partial principles than it ought. The corporation of Boston was not heard before it was condemned. Other towns, full as guilty as she was, have not had their ports blocked up. 35 Even the Restraining Bill of the present session does not go to the length of the Boston Port Act. The same ideas of prudence which induced you not to extend equal punishment to equal guilt, even when you were punishing, induced me, who mean not to chastise but to reconcile, to be satisfied with the punishment already partially inflicted.   5

Ideas of prudence and accommodation to circumstances prevent you from taking away the charters of Connecticut and Rhode Island, as you have taken away that of Massachusetts Colony, though the crown has far less power in the two former provinces than it enjoyed in the latter, and 10 though the abuses have been full as great and as flagrant in the exempted as in the punished. The same reasons of prudence and accommodation have weight with me in restoring the charter of Massachusetts Bay. Besides, Sir, the act which changes the charter of Massachusetts is in many par- 15 ticulars so exceptionable that, if I did not wish absolutely to repeal, I would by all means desire to alter it, as several of its provisions tend to the subversion of all public and private justice. Such, among others, is the power in the governor to change the sheriff at his pleasure, and to make a new 20 returning officer for every special cause. It is shameful to behold such a regulation standing among English laws.

The act for bringing persons accused of committing murder under the orders of government to England for trial is but temporary. That act has calculated the probable 25 duration of our quarrel with the colonies, and is accomo- dated to that supposed duration. I would hasten the happy moment of reconciliation; and therefore must, on my princi- ple, get rid of that most justly obnoxious act.

The act of Henry the Eighth for the trial of treasons I do 30 not mean to take away, but to confine it to its proper bounds and original intention; to make it expressly for trial of treasons (and the greatest treasons may be committed) in places where the jurisdiction of the crown does not extend.

RAMKe

Having guarded the privileges of local legislature, I would next secure to the colonies a fair and unbiased judicature; for which purpose, Sir, I propose the following resolution:—

That, from the time when the general assembly, or general
5 court, of any colony or plantation in North America shall have appointed by act of assembly duly confirmed, a settled salary to the offices of the chief justice and other judges of the superior court, it may be proper that the said chief justice and other judges of the superior courts of such colony shall hold his and their office
10 and offices during their good behavior, and shall not be removed therefrom but when the said removal shall be adjudged by his Majesty in council, upon a hearing on complaint from the general assembly, or on a complaint from the governor or council or the house of representatives, severally, of the colony in which the said
15 chief justice and other judges have exercised the said offices.

The next resolution relates to the courts of admiralty. It is this:—

That it may be proper to regulate the courts of admiralty or vice-admiralty authorized by the fifteenth chapter of the fourth of
20 George the Third, in such a manner as to make the same more commodious to those who sue or are sued in the said courts; and to provide for the more decent maintenance of the judges in the same.

These courts I do not wish to take away: they are in
25 themselves proper establishments. This court is one of the capital securities of the Act of Navigation. The extent of its jurisdiction, indeed, has been increased; but this is alto-gether as proper, and is indeed on many accounts more eligible, where new powers were wanted, than a court abso-
30 lutely new. But courts incommodiously situated in effect deny justice; and a court partaking in the fruits of its own condemnation is a robber. The Congress complain, and complain justly, of this grievance.

These are the three consequential propositions. I have thought of two or three more; but they come rather too near detail and to the province of executive government, which I wish Parliament always to superintend, never to assume. If the first six are granted, congruity will carry the latter three. If not, the things that remain unrepealed will be, I hope, rather unseemly incumbrances on the building than very materially detrimental to its strength and stability.

Here, Sir, I should close; but I plainly perceive some objections remain, which I ought, if possible, to remove. The first will be that, in resorting to the doctrine of our ancestors as contained in the preamble to the Chester Act, I prove too much; that the grievance from a want of representation, stated in that preamble, goes to the whole of legislation as well as to taxation; and that the colonies, grounding themselves upon that doctrine, will apply it to all parts of legislative authority.

To this objection, with all possible deference and humility, and wishing as little as any man living to impair the smallest particle of our supreme authority, I answer that *the words are the words of Parliament, and not mine;* and that all false and inconclusive inferences drawn from them are not mine, for I heartily disclaim any such inference. I have chosen the words of an act of Parliament which Mr. Grenville, surely a tolerably zealous and very judicious advocate for the sovereignty of Parliament, formerly moved to have read at your table in confirmation of his tenets. It is true that Lord Chatham considered these preambles as declaring strongly in favor of his opinions. He was a no less powerful advocate for the privileges of the Americans. Ought I not from hence to presume that these preambles are as favorable as possible to both, when properly understood,—favorable both to the rights of Parliament and to the privilege of the dependencies of this crown? But, Sir, the object of grievance

in my resolution I have not taken from the Chester, but from the Durham Act, which confines the hardship of want of representation to the case of subsidies, and which therefore falls in exactly with the case of the colonies. But
5 whether the unrepresented counties were *de jure* or *de facto* bound, the preambles do not accurately distinguish; nor indeed was it necessary; for whether *de jure* or *de facto*, the legislature thought the exercise of the power of taxing, as of right or as of fact without right, equally a grievance and
10 equally oppressive.

I do not know that the colonies have, in any general way or in any cool hour, gone much beyond the demand of immunity in relation to taxes. It is not fair to judge of the temper or disposition of any man or any set of men, when
15 they are composed and at rest, from their conduct or their expressions in a state of disturbance and irritation. It is, besides, a very great mistake to imagine that mankind follow up practically any speculative principle, either of government or of freedom, as far as it will go in argument
20 and logical illation. We Englishmen stop very short of the principles upon which we support any given part of our Constitution, or even the whole of it together. I could easily, if I had not already tired you, give you very striking and convincing instances of it. This is nothing but what is
25 natural and proper. All government, indeed every human benefit and enjoyment, every virtue, and every prudent act, is founded on compromise and barter. We balance inconveniencies; we give and take; we remit some rights that we may enjoy others; and we choose rather to be happy
30 citizens than subtle disputants. As we must give away some natural liberty to enjoy civil advantages, so we must sacrifice some civil liberties for the advantages to be derived from the communion and fellowship of a great empire. But in all fair dealings the thing bought must bear some propor-

tion to the purchase paid. None will barter away the immediate jewel of his soul. Though a great house is apt to
make slaves haughty, yet it is purchasing a part of the artificial importance of a great empire too dear to pay for it all
essential rights and all the intrinsic dignity of human nature. 5
None of us who would not risk his life rather than fall under
a government purely arbitrary. But although there are
some amongst us who think our Constitution wants many
improvements to make it a complete system of liberty, perhaps none who are of that opinion would think it right to 10
aim at such improvement by disturbing his country and risk-
ing everything that is dear to him. In every arduous enterprise we consider what we are to lose as well as what we
are to gain : and the more and better stake of liberty every
people possess, the less they will hazard in a vain attempt 15
to make it more. These are *the cords of man.* Man acts
from adequate motives relative to his interest, and not on
metaphysical speculations. Aristotle, the great master of
reasoning, cautions us, and with great weight and propriety,
against this species of delusive geometrical accuracy in 20
moral arguments, as the most fallacious of all sophistry.

The Americans will have no interest contrary to the
grandeur and glory of England, when they are not oppressed
by the weight of it ; and they will rather be inclined to respect the acts of a superintending legislature, when they see 25
them the acts of that power which is itself the security, not
the rival, of their secondary importance. In this assurance
my mind most perfectly acquiesces ; and I confess I feel not
the least alarm from the discontents which are to arise from
putting people at their ease ; nor do I apprehend the destruc- 30
tion of this empire from giving, by an act of free grace and
indulgence, to two millions of my fellow-citizens, some share
of those rights upon which I have always been taught to
value myself.

It is said, indeed, that this power of granting, vested in American assemblies, would dissolve the unity of the empire, which was preserved entire, although Wales and Chester and Durham were added to it. Truly, Mr. Speaker, I do not know what this unity means; nor has it ever been heard of, that I know, in the constitutional policy of this country. The very idea of subordination of parts excludes this notion of simple and undivided unity. England is the head, but she is not the head and the members too. Ireland has ever had from the beginning a separate, but not an independent, legislature, which, far from distracting, promoted the union of the whole. Everything was sweetly and harmoniously disposed through both islands for the conservation of English dominion and the communication of English liberties. I do not see that the same principles might not be carried into twenty islands, and with the same good effect. This is my model with regard to America, as far as the internal circumstances of the two countries are the same. I know no other unity of this empire than I can draw from its example during these periods when it seemed to my poor understanding more united than it is now, or than it is likely to be by the present methods.

But since I speak of these methods, I recollect, Mr. Speaker, almost too late, that I promised, before I finished, to say something of the proposition of the noble lord on the floor, which has been so lately received, and stands on your journals. I must be deeply concerned whenever it is my misfortune to continue a difference with the majority of this House. But as the reasons for that difference are my apology for thus troubling you, suffer me to state them in a very few words. I shall compress them into as small a body as I possibly can, having already debated that matter at large when the question was before the committee.

First, then, I cannot admit that proposition of a ransom by auction, because it is a mere project. It is a thing new, unheard of, supported by no experience, justified by no analogy, without example of our ancestors or root in the Constitution. It is neither regular parliamentary taxation nor colony grant. *Experimentum in corpore vili* is a good rule, which will ever make me adverse to any trial of experiments on what is certainly the most valuable of all subjects, —the peace of this empire.

Secondly, it is an experiment which must be fatal in the end to our Constitution. For what is it but a scheme for taxing the colonies in the antechamber of the noble lord and his successors? To settle the quotas and proportions in this House is clearly impossible. You, Sir, may flatter yourself you shall sit a state auctioneer with your hammer in your hand, and knock down to each colony as it bids. But to settle (on the plan laid down by the noble lord) the true proportional payment for four or five and twenty governments, according to the absolute and the relative wealth of each, and according to the British proportion of wealth and burden, is a wild and chimerical notion. This new taxation must therefore come in by the back door of the Constitution. Each quota must be brought to this House ready formed. You can neither add nor alter. You must register it. You can do nothing further. For on what grounds can you deliberate either before or after the proposition? You cannot hear the counsel for all these provinces, quarrelling each on its own quantity of payment and its proportion to others. If you should attempt it, the committee of provincial ways and means, or by whatever other name it will delight to be called, must swallow up all the time of Parliament.

Thirdly, it does not give satisfaction to the complaint of the colonies. They complain that they are taxed without their consent: you answer that you will fix the sum at which

they shall be taxed. That is, you give them the very griev
ance for the remedy.   You tell them, indeed, that you will
leave the mode to themselves.   I really beg pardon ; it
gives me pain to mention it ; but you must be sensible that
5 you will not perform this part of the compact.   For suppose
the colonies were to lay the duties which furnished their
contingent upon the importation of your manufactures, you
know you would never suffer such a tax to be laid.   You
know, too, that you would not suffer many other modes of
10 taxation.   So that when you come to explain yourself, it
will be found that you will neither leave to themselves the
quantum nor the mode ; nor indeed anything.   The whole
is delusion from one end to the other.

Fourthly, this method of ransom by auction, unless it be
15 *universally* accepted, will plunge you into great and inex-
tricable difficulties.   In what year of our Lord are the proportions of payments to be settled?   To say nothing of the
impossibility that colony agents should have general powers
of taxing the colonies at their discretion, consider, I implore
20 you, that the communication by special messages and orders
between these agents and their constituents on each variation
of the case, when the parties come to contend together and
to dispute on their relative proportions, will be a matter of
delay, perplexity and confusion that never can have an
25 end.

If all the colonies do not appear at the outcry, what is the
condition of those assemblies who offer, by themselves or
their agents, to tax themselves up to your ideas of their
proportion ?   The refractory colonies who refuse all com-
30 position will remain taxed only to your old impositions,
which, however grievous in principle, are trifling as to production.   The obedient colonies in this scheme are heavily
taxed ; the refractory remain unburdened.   What will you
do ?   Will you lay new and heavier taxes by Parliament on

the disobedient? Pray consider in what way you can do it. You are perfectly convinced that in the way of taxing you can do nothing but at the ports. Now suppose it is Virginia that refuses to appear at your auction, while Maryland and North Carolina bid handsomely for their ransom, and are taxed to your quota, how will you put these colonies on a par? Will you tax the tobacco of Virginia? If you do, you give its death-wound to your English revenue at home and to one of the very greatest articles of your own foreign trade. If you tax the import of that rebellious colony, what do you tax but your own manufactures or the goods of some other obedient and already well-taxed colony? Who has said one word on this labyrinth of detail which bewilders you more and more as you enter into it? Who has presented, who can present you with a clue to lead you out of it? I think, Sir, it is impossible that you should not recollect that the colony bounds are so implicated in one another (you know it by your other experiments in the bill for prohibiting the New England fishery) that you can lay no possible restraints on almost any of them which may not be presently eluded, if you do not confound the innocent with the guilty, and burden those whom, upon every principle, you ought to exonerate. He must be grossly ignorant of America who thinks that, without falling into this confusion of all rules of equity and policy, you can restrain any single colony, especially Virginia and Maryland, the central and most important of them all.

Let it also be considered that, either in the present confusion you settle a permanent contingent, which will and must be trifling, and then you have no effectual revenue ; or you change the quota at every exigency, and then on every new repartition you will have a new quarrel.

Reflect besides, that when you have fixed a quota for every colony, you have not provided for prompt and punctual payment.   Suppose one, two, five, ten years' arrears.   You cannot issue a treasury extent against the failing colony. You must make new Boston Port Bills, new restraining laws, new acts for dragging men to England for trial.   You must send out new fleets, new armies.   All is to begin again. From this day forward the empire is never to know an hour's tranquillity.   An intestine fire will be kept alive in the bowels of the colonies, which one time or other must consume this whole empire.   I allow indeed that the empire of Germany raises her revenue and her troops by quotas and contingents; but the revenue of the empire and the army of the empire is the worst revenue and the worst army in the world.

Instead of a standing revenue, you will therefore have a perpetual quarrel.   Indeed, the noble lord who proposed this project of a ransom by auction seemed himself to be of that opinion.   His project was rather designed for breaking the union of the colonies than for establishing a revenue. He confessed he apprehended that his proposal would not be to *their taste*.   I say this scheme of disunion seems to be at the bottom of the project ; for I will not suspect that the noble lord meant nothing but merely to delude the nation by an airy phantom which he never intended to realize. But whatever his views may be, as I propose the peace and union of the colonies as the very foundation of my plan, it cannot accord with one whose foundation is perpetual discord.

Compare the two.   This I offer to give you is plain and simple : the other full of perplexed and intricate mazes. This is mild : that harsh.   This is found by experience effectual for its purposes: the other is a new project.   This is universal : the other calculated for certain colonies only. This is immediate in its conciliatory operation : the other remote, contingent, full of hazard.   Mine is what becomes

What is the debt of the. W. I ?

THE POWER OF REFUSAL. 69

the dignity of a ruling people, — gratuitous, unconditional, and not held out as a matter of bargain and sale. I have done my duty in proposing it to you. I have indeed tired you by a long discourse; but this is the misfortune of those to whose influence nothing will be conceded, and who must 5 win every inch of their ground by argument. You have heard me with goodness. May you decide with wisdom! For my part, I feel my mind greatly disburdened by what I have done to-day. I have been the less fearful of trying your patience, because on this subject I mean to spare it 10 altogether in future. I have this comfort, that in every stage of the American affairs I have steadily opposed the measures that have produced the confusion, and may bring on the destruction, of this empire. I now go so far as to risk a proposal of my own. If I cannot give peace to my 15 country, I give it to my conscience.

131 "But what," says the financier, "is peace to us without money? Your plan gives us no revenue." No! But it does; for it secures to the subject the power of REFUSAL, the first of all revenues. Experience is a cheat and fact a 20 liar, if this power in the subject of proportioning his grant, or of not granting at all, has not been found the richest mine of revenue ever discovered by the skill or by the fortune of man. It does not indeed vote you £152,750 11s. 2¾ths, nor any other paltry limited sum; but it gives the strong-box 25 itself, the fund, the bank, from whence only revenues can arise amongst a people sensible of freedom: *Posita luditur arca.* Cannot you in England, cannot you at this time of day, cannot you, an House of Commons, trust to the principle which has raised so mighty a revenue and accumulated a 30 debt of near 140 millions in this country? Is this principle to be true in England and false everywhere else? Is it not true in Ireland? Has it not hitherto been true in the colonies? Why should you presume that in any country a body

duly constituted for any function will neglect to perform its duty and abdicate its trust? Such a presumption would go against all governments in all modes. But in truth this dread of penury of supply from a free assembly has no foundation in nature. For first observe, that besides the desire which all men have naturally of supporting the honor of their own government, that sense of dignity and that security to property which ever attends freedom has a tendency to increase the stock of the free community. Most may be taken where most is accumulated. And what is the soil or climate where experience has not uniformly proved that the voluntary flow of heaped-up plenty, bursting from the weight of its own rich luxuriance, has ever run with a more copious stream of revenue than could be squeezed from the dry husks of oppressed indigence by the straining of all the politic machinery in the world?

Next, we know that parties must ever exist in a free country. We know, too, that the emulations of such parties, their contradictions, their reciprocal necessities, their hopes and their fears, must send them all in their turns to him that holds the balance of the state. The parties are the gamesters; but government keeps the table, and is sure to be the winner in the end. When this game is played, I really think it is more to be feared that the people will be exhausted than that government will not be supplied. Whereas, whatever is got by acts of absolute power, ill obeyed because odious, or by contracts ill kept because constrained, will be narrow, feeble, uncertain and precarious.

> Ease would retract
> Vows made in pain, as violent and void.

I, for one, protest against compounding our demands : I declare against compounding for a poor limited sum the immense, ever-growing, eternal debt which is due to gen-

erous government from protected freedom. And so may I
speed in the great object I propose to you, as I think it
would not only be an act of injustice, but would be the worst
economy in the world, to compel the colonies to a sum certain, either in the way of ransom or in the way of compulsory 5
compact.

But to clear up my ideas on this subject, — a revenue
from America transmitted hither, — do not delude yourselves : you never can receive it, — no, not a shilling. We
have experience that from remote countries it is not to be 10
expected. If, when you attempted to extract revenue from
Bengal, you were obliged to return in loan what you had
taken in imposition, what can you expect from North
America ? For certainly, if ever there was a country qualified to produce wealth, it is India ; or an institution fit for 15
the transmission, it is the East India Company. America has
none of these aptitudes. If America gives you taxable objects on which you lay your duties here, and gives you at
the same time a surplus by a foreign sale of her commodities to pay the duties on these objects which you tax at 20
home, she has performed her part to the British revenue.
But with regard to her own internal establishments, she may,
— I doubt not she will, — contribute in moderation. I say
in moderation ; for she ought not to be permitted to exhaust
herself. She ought to be reserved to a war, the weight of 25
which, with the enemies that we are most likely to have,
must be considerable in her quarter of the globe. There
she may serve you, and serve you essentially.

For that service, for all service, whether of revenue, trade
or empire, my trust is in her interest in the British Constitu- 30
tion. My hold of the colonies is in the close affection which
grows from common names, from kindred blood, from similar privileges and equal protection. These are ties which,
though light as air, are as strong as links of iron. Let the

colonies always keep the idea of their civil rights associated with your government, — they will cling and grapple to you, and no force under heaven will be of power to tear them from their allegiance.   But let it be once understood that
5 your government may be one thing and their privileges another ; that these two things may exist without any mutual relation, the cement is gone, the cohesion is loosened and everything hastens to decay and dissolution.   As long as you have the wisdom to keep the sovereign authority of
10 this country as the sanctuary of liberty, the sacred temple consecrated to our common faith, wherever the chosen race and sons of England worship freedom, they will turn their faces towards you.   The more they multiply, the more friends you will have ; the more ardently they love liberty,
15 the more perfect will be their obedience.   Slavery they can have anywhere.   It is a weed that grows in every soil.   They may have it from Spain ; they may have it from Prussia. But until you become lost to all feeling of your true interest and your natural dignity, freedom they can have from none
20 but you.   This is the commodity of price, of which you have the monopoly.   This is the true Act of Navigation which binds to you the commerce of the colonies, and through them secures to you the wealth of the world.   Deny them this participation of freedom, and you break that sole bond
25 which originally made and must still preserve the unity of the empire.   Do not entertain so weak an imagination as that your registers and your bonds, your affidavits and your sufferances, your cockets and your clearances, are what form the great securities of your commerce.   Do not dream that
30 your letters of office and your instructions and your suspend- ing clauses are the things that hold together the great con- texture of the mysterious whole.   These things do not make your government.   Dead instruments, passive tools as they are, it is the spirit of the English communion that gives all

their life and efficacy to them. It is the spirit of the English Constitution, which, infused through the mighty mass, pervades, feeds, unites, invigorates, vivifies every part of the empire, even down to the minutest member.

Is it not the same virtue which does everything for us here 5 in England? Do you imagine, then, that it is the Land Tax Act which raises your revenue? that it is the annual vote in the Committee of Supply which gives you your army? or that it is the Mutiny Bill which inspires it with bravery and discipline? No! surely no! It is the love of the people: 10 it is their attachment to their government, from the sense of the deep stake they have in such a glorious institution, which gives you your army and your navy, and infuses into both that liberal obedience without which your army would be a base rabble, and your navy nothing but rotten timber. 15

All this, I know well enough, will sound wild and chimerical to the profane herd of those vulgar and mechanical politicians who have no place among us, — a sort of people who think that nothing exists but what is gross and material; and who, therefore, far from being qualified to be directors 20 of the great movement of empire, are not fit to turn a wheel in the machine. But to men truly initiated and rightly taught, these ruling and master principles, which in the opinion of such men as I have mentioned have no substantial existence, are in truth everything and all in all. Mag- 25 nanimity in politics is not seldom the truest wisdom; and a great empire and little minds go ill together. If we are conscious of our situation and glow with zeal to fill our places as becomes our station and ourselves, we ought to auspicate all our public proceedings on America with the old warning 30 of the church, *Sursum corda!* We ought to elevate our minds to the greatness of that trust to which the order of Providence has called us. By adverting to the dignity of this high calling, our ancestors have turned a savage wilder-

ness into a glorious empire ; and have made the most extensive, and the only honorable conquests, not by destroying, but by promoting the wealth, the number, the happiness of the human race.   Let us get an American revenue as we
5 have got an American empire.   English privileges have made it all that it is ; English privileges alone will make it all it can be.

In full confidence of this unalterable truth, I now (*quod felix faustumque sit!*) lay the first stone of the Temple of
10 Peace ; and I move you, —

That the colonies and plantations of Great Britain in North America, consisting of fourteen separate governments, and containing two millions and upwards of free inhabitants, have not had the liberty and privilege of electing and sending any knights and
15 burgesses, or others, to represent them in the high court of Parliament.

———————

Upon this resolution the previous question was put and carried : for the previous question, 270 ; against it, 78.

As the propositions were opened separately in the body
20 of the speech, the reader perhaps may wish to see the whole of them together in the form in which they were moved for. The first four motions and the last had the previous question put on them.   The others were negatived.   The words in italics were, by an amendment that was carried, left out of
25 the motion.

Moved,

That the colonies and plantations of Great Britain in North America, consisting of fourteen separate governments, and containing two millions and upwards of free inhabitants, have not had
30 the liberty and privilege of electing and sending any knights and burgesses, or others, to represent them in the high court of Parliament.

That the said colonies and plantations have been made liable to, and bounden by, several subsidies, payments, rates and taxes, given and granted by Parliament, though the said colonies and plantations have not their knights and burgesses in the said high court of Parliament, of their own election, to represent the condition of 5 their country ; *by lack whereof they have been oftentimes touched and grieved by subsidies given, granted and assented to, in the said court, in a manner prejudicial to the commonwealth, quietness, rest and peace of the subjects inhabiting within the same.*

That, from the distance of the said colonies and from other 10 circumstances, no method hath hitherto been devised for procuring a representation in Parliament for the said colonies.

That each of the said colonies hath within itself a body, chosen in part or in the whole by the freemen, freeholders or other free inhabitants thereof, commonly called the general assembly, or 15 general court ; with powers legally to raise, levy and assess, according to the several usage of such colonies, duties and taxes towards defraying all sorts of public services.

That the said general assemblies, general courts, or other bodies legally qualified as aforesaid, have at sundry times freely granted 20 several large subsidies and public aids for his Majesty's service, according to their abilities, when required thereto by letter from one of his Majesty's principal secretaries of state ; and that their right to grant the same and their cheerfulness and sufficiency in the said grants have been at sundry times acknowledged by 25 Parliament.

That it hath been found by experience that the manner of granting the said supplies and aids by the said general assemblies hath been more agreeable to the inhabitants of the said colonies, and more beneficial and conducive to the public service, than the 30 mode of giving and granting aids in Parliament, to be raised and paid in the said colonies.

That it may be proper to repeal an act made in the seventh year of the reign of his present Majesty, entitled, "An act for granting certain duties in the British colonies and plantations in 35

America ; for allowing a drawback of the duties of customs upon the exportation from this kingdom, of coffee and cocoanuts of the produce of the said colonies or plantations ; for discontinuing the drawbacks payable on China earthenware exported to America ;
5 and for more effectually preventing the clandestine running of goods in the said colonies and plantations."

That it may be proper to repeal an act made in the fourteenth year of the reign of his present Majesty, entitled, " An act to discontinue, in such manner and for such time as are therein mentioned,
10 the landing and discharging, lading or shipping, of goods, wares and merchandise, at the town and within the harbor of Boston, in the province of Massachusetts Bay, in North America."

That it may be proper to repeal an act made in the fourteenth year of the reign of his present Majesty, entitled, " An act for the
15 impartial administration of justice in the cases of persons questioned for any acts done by them in the execution of the law, or for the suppression of riots and tumults, in the province of Massachusetts Bay, in New England."

That it may be proper to repeal an act made in the fourteenth
20 year of the reign of his present Majesty, entitled, " An act for the better regulating the government of the province of the Massachusetts Bay, in New England."

That it may be proper to explain and amend an act made in the thirty-fifth year of the reign of King Henry the Eighth,
25 entitled, " An act for the trial of treasons committed out of the king's dominions."

That from the time when the general assembly, or general court, of any colony or plantation in North America shall have appointed by act of assembly duly confirmed, a settled salary to
30 the offices of the chief justice and other judges of the superior court, it may be proper that the said chief justice and other judges of the superior courts of such colony shall hold his and their office and offices during their good behavior, and shall not be removed therefrom but when the said removal shall be adjudged by his
35 Majesty in council, upon a hearing on complaint from the general

assembly, **or** on a complaint from the governor or council or the house of representatives, severally, of the colony in which the said chief justice and other judges have exercised the said offices.

That it may be proper to regulate the courts of admiralty or vice-admiralty authorized by the fifteenth chapter of the fourth of 5 George the Third, in such a manner as to make the same more commodious to those who sue or are sued in the said courts ; *and to provide for the more decent maintenance of the judges of the same.*

NOTES.

———◆———

References to passages in Burke's other writings are to the twelve-volume edition of the *Works* (abbreviation *W.*), Little, Brown and Company, Boston, 1894; and to the four volumes of the *Correspondence* (*C.*), Rivington, London, 1844. Both sets of books, especially the first, are desirable for the reference library of any school where Burke is studied. References to Dodsley's *Annual Register* are marked *A.R.*; those to the *Parliamentary History*, London, 1806–1820, *P.H.*, and unless otherwise noted are to volume XVIII; those to the *Dictionary of National Biography*, *D.N.B.* References to Bancroft are to the *History of the United States*, six volumes, Appleton, New York, 1888; to Lecky, *England in the Eighteenth Century*, eight volumes, Appleton, New York, 1878–1890; to Green, *History of the English People*, four volumes, Harper, New York, 1880; to *Journals of the American Congress*, the edition published at Washington, 1823. References to volumes are in capital Roman numerals; to chapters or similar subdivisions, in small Roman.

3 1. **Sir, that notwithstanding the austerity of the Chair.** In the House of Commons and similar bodies speeches are nominally addressed, not to the members, but to the presiding officer, called the Speaker, the Chairman, or often the Chair. Instances of this form of address are found in the following passages: 10 27–29 and 28 17. The Speaker at this time was Sir Fletcher Norton, who held the office from 1770 to 1780. Any one interested in his career may study it in the *Dictionary of National Biography*. He is bitterly attacked in letter xxxix of Junius. The phrase *austerity of the Chair* refers to the fact that in impartially preserving order the Speaker is necessarily austere and sometimes even severe.

3 7. **event.** Result. **my motion.** The motion made at the end of the speech.

3 8. **grand penal bill.** A bill to prevent the New England colonies from trading with any countries except Great Britain, Ireland, and the British Islands in the West Indies; and to prohibit the colonies from the Newfoundland fisheries except under certain conditions. When Lord North brought in this bill, February 10, 1775 (*P.H.*, 299), he defended it on the ground that, because the Americans refused to trade with England, England should not suffer them to trade with any other nation. Burke

replied (*ibid.*, 304) that the bill by destroying the source of the colonists' income would make it impossible for them to pay their large debts to English merchants and manufacturers. The bill came up again February 24 and 28 and March 6. On the last of these days Burke attacked it again (*ibid.*, 389), declaring that it attempted to preserve authority by destroying dominion; and that it passed sentence of beggary, if not famine, on four great provinces. In another debate on May 8, when the bill was passed, Burke said (*ibid.*, 396) that it "did not mean to shed blood; but, to suit some gentleman's humanity, it only meant to starve five hundred thousand people." For an account of the bill and the debates on it, see *P. H.*, 298–305, 379–400, 421–461. For another good account, perhaps written by Burke himself, see *A. R.*, 1775, chapter vi. Since chapters i to viii all deal with American affairs, they contain much matter of interest in connection with this speech.

3 10. returned to us from the other House. The House of Lords thought the provisions of the bill might well be extended to New Jersey, Pennsylvania, Maryland, Virginia, and South Carolina, and therefore returned it to the Commons for amendment. See *P. H.*, 455–458.

3 13. once more in possession of our deliberative capacity. On the return of the bill the Commons could again discuss it.

3 18. first day. November 29, 1774. *P. H.*, 1.

3 21. mixture of coerçion and restraint. The coercion was the attempt to crush the resistance of New England to the tea duty; the restraint, the restrictions upon trade. Such a "mixture" is not "incongruous" in itself, but is "incongruous" with "conciliation."

4 2. first. In 1765 Burke was elected to Parliament as member for the borough of Wendover, but he did not take his seat till early in 1766.

4 4. delicate. Requiring careful treatment. Compare, "These delicate points ought to be wholly left to the crown." *Letter to the Sheriffs of Bristol, W.*, II, 222.

4 8. trust. The idea that powers of government are held in trust for the people comes out again and again in Burke's writings. Compare the following passages: "They [Parliament and the crown] all are trustees for the people." *Thoughts on the Cause of the Present Discontents, W.*, I, 492. "I had . . . very earnest wishes to keep the whole body of this authority perfect . . . principally for the sake of those on whose account all just authority exists: I mean the people to be governed." *Letter to the Sheriffs of Bristol, W.*, II, 223, 224.

4 9. more than common pains. Burke had in 1757 written, or helped to write, an *Account of the European Settlements in America,* and since that date his work in Parliament and on the *Annual Register* had kept him thoroughly informed on American affairs. As a result, he probably knew more about the subject than any one in England. In his *Letter to the Sheriffs of Bristol, W.,* II, 209, he says: "I think I know America. — If I do not, my ignorance is incurable, for I have spared no pains to understand it."

4 16. blown about by every wind of fashionable doctrine. Compare, "Henceforth be no more children, tossed to and fro, and carried about with every wind of doctrine." *Ephesians,* iv, 14.

4 18. fresh principles. Burke is constantly urging the necessity of more fixed principles in public policy. For example, in a letter to Charles James Fox, October 8, 1777, he says: "I have ever wished a settled plan of our own, founded in the very essence of the American business, wholly unconnected with the events of the war." *W.,* VI, 137. See also 26 7.

4 20. that period. In 1766 Parliament was inclined to conciliate the colonies, and so repealed the Stamp Act by a vote of 275 to 161. See *P. H.,* XVI, 161–206; and *A. R.,* 1766, chapter viii.

4 29. more frequent changes. See Introduction, xv–xviii.

5 3. complaint. Disease.

5 10. a worthy member. Mr. Rose Fuller, member for Rye. It was during a debate on April 19, 1774, on a motion by Mr. Fuller to repeal the American tea duty, that Burke made what is known as the *Speech on American Taxation.* See *W.,* II, 5; and *P. H.,* XVII, 1210–1273.

5 11. filled the Chair of the American Committee. Presided when the whole House sat as a committee on American affairs.

5 14. our former methods. Both Burke and Fuller belonged to the minority which had been criticising the action of the majority in regard to America.

5 26. produce our hand. Show the cards in our hand; that is, set forth our own policy. The prevalence of gambling in Burke's day made allusions to it more natural than they would be now. See 69 27, 70 22, 23; also *George Selwyn and His Contemporaries,* London, 1843, I, 18, 27, 28.

5 30. platform. Outline, ground plan.

6 4. gave so far into his opinion. Compare, "This [the natural slavery of barbarians] was so general a notion, that Aristotle himself, with all his penetration, *gave into* it very seriously." *European Settlements in America,* London, 1757, I, 31. (Payne.)

6 10. disreputably. To the damage of the reputation of those who make them.

6 15. paper government. Burke's contempt for a plan based on theory rather than experience is often strongly expressed, not only in this speech, but throughout his writings. Compare 9 30–34, 18 28, 41 24, 49 16–18, 65 3;

also the following passages : " It is proposed merely as a project of speculative improvement." *Present State of the Nation, W.*, I, 372. " I reprobate
no form of government merely upon abstract principles." *Reflections on
the Revolution in France*, III, 396. " But the practice and knowledge of
the world will not suffer us to be ignorant that the Constitution on paper
is one thing, and in fact and experience is another." *Speech on the Duration of Parliaments*, VII, 77.

6 24. **most inconsiderable person.** Compare, " When the affairs of
the nation are distracted, private people are . . . justified in stepping a little
out of their ordinary sphere." *Thoughts on the Cause of the Present Discontents, W.*, I, 435.

7 4. **natural.** Arising from natural, or inborn, abilities. **adventitious.**
Due to external causes, such as rank or wealth.

7 13. **discord fomented from principle.** On February 20, 1775, Lord
North brought in a resolution (*P. H.*, 319) that when any colony made
proper provision for contributing its proportion for the common defence
and for maintaining civil government, Parliament should no longer levy
taxes on it, except for the regulation of commerce. In the course of the
debate Colonel Barré said (*ibid.*, 333) : " Though the noble lord's new
motion will cause no new divisions amongst us here, yet it is founded on
that wretched, low, shameful, abominable maxim which has predominated
in every measure of our late minister, *divide et impera.* This is to divide
the Americans ; this is to break those associations, to dissolve that generous union in which the Americans, as one man, stand in defence of their
rights and liberties." Lord North answered (334) : " The gentleman has
charged me with mean, low and foolish policy in grounding my measures
on that maxim, *divide et impera.* Is it foolish, is it mean, when a people,
heated and misled by evil councils, are running into unlawful combina-
tions, to hold out those terms which will sift the reasonable from the
unreasonable ? that will distinguish those who act upon principle from
those who only wish to profit of the general confusion ? If propositions
that the conscientious and the prudent will accept will at the same time
recover them from the influence and fascination of the wicked, I avow the
using that principle which will thus divide the good from the bad, and give
support to the friends of peace and good government." Later in the
debate Mr. Temple Luttrell asked (349) : " What is the aim and scope of
the resolution ? To lure some of the less refractory provinces of America
to dissociate from and betray their fellow-sufferers ; to join in raising a
contribution throughout one half of the colonies to support your armaments
and outrages against the other half, with a view to annihilate trade, cut off
every natural channel of livelihood and subsistence, and butcher the dis-

obedient ; and how are these seceders to be recompensed for such signal perfidy ?" For a full account of this debate, to which Burke evidently alludes, see *P. H.*, 319–358, and *A. R.*, 1775, chapter vii. See also 68 17–21.

7 14. **juridical determination.** *Juridical* is sometimes used as if exactly synonymous with *judicial.* The latter, according to the *Century Dictionary*, means pertaining to a judge, proper to the character of a judge, pertaining to the administration of justice : *juridical*, however, means founded upon. or in accordance with the strict forms of law, or abstract legal conceptions, rather than with general principles of justice. A *juridical determination* is one which might be reached on purely legal grounds, according to the technical forms of law. The idea that an act of government should be based not so much on strict legal forms as on a broad policy of reason and justice, is a favorite one with Burke, and is frequently urged in this and other speeches. Compare 37 26, 38 14 ; also, " Men of sense, when new projects come before them, always think a discourse proving the mere right or mere power of acting in the manner proposed, to be no more than a very unpleasant way of misspending time." *Present State of the Nation, W.*, I, 367. " Those reasonings which infer from the many restraints under which we have already laid America to our right to lay it under still more, and indeed under all manner of restraints, are conclusive ; conclusive as to right ; but the very reverse as to policy and practice." *Ibid.*, 396. " Whether all this can be reconciled in legal speculation is a matter of no consequence. It is reconciled in policy : and politics ought to be adjusted, not to human reasonings, but to human nature." 398.

7 16. **boundaries.** Not geographical boundaries, but limits of power, — especially in regard to taxing, the question in dispute. Compare, " I am not here going into distinctions of rights nor attempting to mark their boundaries." *Speech on American Taxation, W.*, II, 73.

7 21. **unsuspecting confidence.** These words refer to a passage in a declaration by the Continental Congress, which met at Philadelphia, September 5, 1774. On October 21 this Congress issued two addresses, one to Great Britain and one to the colonies. In the latter occurs the following paragraph : " After the repeal of the Stamp Act, having again resigned ourselves to our ancient unsuspicious affections for the parent state, and anxious to avoid any controversy with her, in hopes of a favorable alteration in sentiments and measures towards us, we did not press our objections against the above-mentioned statutes made subsequent to that repeal." *Journals of Congress*, I, 33. In the *Letter to the Sheriffs of Bristol*, 1777, Burke, in speaking of the Stamp Act, again brings up this declaration : " After the repeal of the Stamp Act, ' the colonies fell,' says this assembly,

'into their ancient state of *unsuspecting confidence in the mother country.*
This unsuspecting confidence is the true centre of gravity amongst mankind, about which all the parts are at rest. It is this *unsuspecting confidence* that removes all difficulties and reconciles all the contradictions
which occur in the complexity of all ancient puzzled political establishments. Happy are the rulers which have the secret of preserving it !"
W., II, 234.

7 26. **Refined.** Fine-spun, elaborate. Compare, "This fine-spun scheme
had the usual fate of all exquisite policy." *American Taxation, W.*, II, 68.

8 1. **pruriency.** The primary meaning is *itching ;* the secondary, *desire*, or *appetite.* The word is always used in a bad sense.

8 3. **project.** See 7 13, note. This resolution moved by Lord North
was finally passed, February 27.

8 4. **noble lord.** Lord North : born 1732 ; Prime Minister from 1770
to 1782 ; died 1792. He steadily opposed all concessions to the Americans, though it is said that in this mistaken policy he often followed the
king's judgment rather than his own. He has been so bitterly attacked by
all partisans of America, that few of us are aware that he was able and
fluent in debate ; that he had a remarkably quick wit and a temper which
scarcely anything could ruffle ; and that in all private intercourse he was
scrupulously honorable. An interesting sketch of his character may be
found in Brougham's *Statesmen of the Time of George the Third*, First
Series. For the best short account of his life, see *D. N. B.* The presence
of a so-called *lord* in the House of Commons is due to the custom of giving
a title by courtesy to the eldest son of a peer while the father is yet living.
blue ribbon. The badge of a Knight of the Garter, to which order Lord
North had belonged since 1772. Though the order was instituted in 1344,
the honor of membership has been bestowed on only three other com-
moners, Sir Robert Walpole, Lord Castlereagh, and Lord Palmerston.

8 5. **colony agents.** The colonies had agents in England to look after
their interests. At one time Franklin, for example, was agent for Pennsylvania, Massachusetts, Maryland, and Georgia.

8 6. **mace.** The sergeant-at-arms, the executive officer of the House,
bears a mace as the sign of his authority.

8 8. **auction of finance.** See 65 15. When Lord North introduced his
resolution, February 20, 1775, Burke is reported as saying during the
debate : " They [the colonists] are to be held prisoners of war, unless they
consent to a ransom by bidding at an auction against each other and
against themselves, until the king and Parliament shall strike down the
hammer and say, 'Enough.' This species of auction, to be terminated,
not at the discretion of the bidder, but at the will of the sovereign power,

is a kind of absurd tyranny which I challenge the ministers to produce any example of in the practice of this or of any other nation." *P. H.,* 336. In the report of the debate in *A. R.,* *100, this sentence occurs: " The House is to be converted into an auction room, the Speaker to hold the hammer."

8 18. **address.** February 9, 1775, the houses of Parliament had presented to the king a joint address on the disturbances in America, declaring that no part of the sovereign authority over the colonies should be relinquished, and closing with this sentence: " We consider it as our indispensable duty humbly to beseech your Majesty that you will take the most effectual measures to enforce due obedience to the laws and authority of the supreme legislature ; and we beg leave in the most solemn manner to assure your Majesty that it is our fixed resolution, at the hazard of our lives and properties, to stand by your Majesty against all rebellious attempts, in the maintenance of the just rights of your Majesty and the two houses of Parliament." *P. H.,* 297, 298.

8 19. **bill.** See 3 8. In the debate in the House of Lords, March 16, Lord Shelburne said that "he entirely coincided in sentiments with the noble lord [Camden] who called this a bill of pains, penalties, and coercion." *P. H.,* 448.

8 20. **grace and bounty.** Lord North's resolutions were entitled *Propositions for Conciliating the Differences with America. P. H.,* 319. In the course of the debate Lord North referred to "the idea of the indulgence which the address held out," and said the same idea appeared in his propositions. 334. In the report in *A. R.,* *95, he is made to say that Parliament meant to show its "tenderness and conciliatory disposition."

8 22. **previous to any submission.** On February 6, during a debate on the address to the king touching the disturbances in North America, Mr. Hans Stanley " said he wanted nothing but the Americans to submit ; would then hang out the olive branch, propose an amnesty, an act of grace and oblivion." *P. H.,* 248. On February 27, Mr. Ackland expressed the same view. 340.

8 29. **capital.** Important or fundamental. Compare 9 19, 23 31.

9 31. **that nature and those circumstances.** Compare, "A statesman, never losing sight of principles, is to be guided by circumstances ; and judging contrary to the exigencies of the moment, he may ruin his country forever." *Speech on the Petition of the Unitarians, W.,* VII, 41. "The happiness or misery of mankind, estimated by their feelings and sentiments and not by any theories of their rights, is, and ought to be, the standard for the conduct of legislators towards the people." *Ibid.,* 45.

9 33. **mere general theories.** Compare 6 15, note.

10 9. two millions. Bancroft (II, 390) puts the number in 1770 as 1,850,000 whites and 462,000 blacks, total, 2,312,000; in 1780, as 2,383,000 whites, 562,000 blacks, total, 2,945,000. Lecky says the number of whites slightly exceeded two millions at the time of the Declaration of Independence. III, 290. Burke's estimate for 1775 seems, therefore, to be pretty accurate.

10 30. occasional. Designed merely for the occasion. See 4 18, note; 18 5. Compare, " Sir, it is not a pleasant consideration, but nothing in the world can read so awful and so instructive a lesson as the conduct of ministry in this business, upon the mischief of not having large and liberal ideas in the management of great affairs. Never have the servants of the state looked at the whole of your complicated interests in one connected view. They have taken things by bits and scraps, some at one time and one pretence, and some at another, just as they pressed, without any sort of regard to their relations or dependencies. They never had any kind of system, right or wrong; but only invented occasionally some miserable tale for the day in order meanly to sneak out of difficulties into which they had proudly strutted." *Speech on American Taxation, W.,* II, 14.

10 32. minima. A reference to the maxim, *De minimis non curat lex,* the law takes no account of trifles.

11 4. so large a mass. Compare, " This consideration of the magnitude of the object ought to attend us through the whole inquiry : if it does not always affect the reason, it is always decisive on the importance of the question." *Tract on the Popery Laws, W.,* VI, 319.

✗✗✗ **11 13. some days ago.** March 16. The American Congress, which met in Philadelphia in the autumn of 1774, passed a resolution October 20, declaring that to obtain redress of grievances a non-importation agreement was necessary, under the terms of which the colonies should not import any goods from Great Britain or Ireland, and should not import " molasses, syrups, paneles, coffee, or pimento " from the West Indies. *Journals of Congress,* I, 23. Alarmed at this threat, the West India planters presented to Parliament, February 2, 1775, a petition " praying the House to take into their most serious consideration that great political system of the colonies heretofore so very beneficial to the mother country and her dependencies, and adopt such measures as to them shall seem meet to prevent the evils with which the petitioners are threatened, and to preserve the intercourse between the West India Islands and the northern colonies, to the general harmony and lasting benefit of the whole British Empire." *P. H.,* 219–221. On March 16 Mr. Richard Glover appeared for the petitioners and discussed in detail the trade of the colonies. *Ibid.,* 461–478.

11 14. **distinguished person.** Mr. Glover, who was born in 1712, published in 1737 *Leonidas*, an epic in nine books, which gave him great reputation at the time, and which was often reprinted during the eighteenth century. In 1787, two years after his death, another epic of his, the *Athenaid*, was published. One of his popular ballads, *Admiral Hosier's Ghost*, is in book vi of Percy's *Reliques*. In 1761 he was elected to Parliament. Nineteen years before, however, he had appeared before the House in behalf of the merchants of London, who had petitioned for the protection of their commerce from the Spanish privateers. The petition was presented January 20, 1742, and January 27 Mr. Glover summed up the evidence in the matter. Since 1742 is the date in *D. N. B.*, XXII, 6, and in the *History and Proceedings of the House of Commons*, Chandler, London, 1743, XXII, 109, it is to be inferred, as Cook notes, that Burke, speaking in 1775, should have said *thirty-three* instead of *thirty-five* years. **bar.** A rod across the entrance to the chamber of Parliament. Members and officers only are admitted within.

11 32. **state.** Statement. Compare, " They who are inclined to think favorably of that event [the French Revolution] will undoubtedly object to every *state* of facts which comes only from the authority of a royalist." *Preface to Brissot's Address, W.*, V, 67.

12 5. **on your table.** Officially presented to the House.

12 6. **Davenant.** Charles Davenant: born, 1656; appointed inspector-general of exports and imports, 1705; died, 1714. He was a writer on economics, author of *Discourses on Revenue and Trade*. See *D. N. B.*

12 10. **terminating almost wholly in the colonies.** English wares were carried to Africa and exchanged for slaves who were sold in the colonies.

13 32. **It is good for us to be here.** Compare *Matthew*, xvii, 1–4 : " And after six days Jesus taketh Peter, James, and John his brother, and bringeth them up into a high mountain apart, and was transfigured before them : and his face did shine as the sun, and his raiment was white as the light. And behold, there appeared unto them Moses and Elias talking with him. Then answered Peter, and said unto Jesus, ' Lord, it is good for us to be here.' "

14 7. **Lord Bathurst.** Allen Bathurst: born, 1684; made Baron Bathurst, 1712. After his son Henry was in 1771 made Lord Chancellor, the highest judicial officer of the crown, the father was in 1772 raised to the rank of earl. He was a friend of Pope, Swift, Prior, and the other wits of the reign of Queen Anne. He died in September, 1775, six months after this speech. See *D. N. B.*

14 10. **acta parentum.** He was able to study the deeds of his fore-

fathers and to learn what virtue is.   Altered from Virgil's *Eclogues*, iv,
26, 27 :

Facta parentis
Jam legere et quae sit poteris cognoscere virtus.

14 11.   **auspicious.**   Favored.

14 14.   **fourth generation the third prince.**   George the Second was
succeeded by his grandson George the Third, who thus belonged to the
fourth generation.

14 16.   **twelve years.**   George the Third came to the throne in 1760.

14 17.   **was to be made.**   It was not until 1707 that the Act of Union
made England and Scotland one nation.

14 20.   **fountain.**   The sovereign, who bestows titles of nobility, is
represented as the *fountain of hereditary dignities*.

14 31.   **taste of death.**   Compare *Matthew*, xvi, 28 : " There be some
standing here, which shall not taste of death till they see the Son of man
coming in his kingdom."   *John*, viii, 52 : " If a man keep my saying, he
shall never taste of death."   Shakspere's *Julius Caesar*, act ii, scene 2, 33 :
" The valiant never taste of death but once."

15 29.   **Deceive.**   A Latinism: the Latin *fallere* — deceive — sometimes
means to cause anything not to be observed or felt, to lighten anything
difficult.   Compare Horace, *Satires*, ii, 7, 114 : " Jam somno fallere
curam," by sleep to lighten care.   Ovid, *Tristia*, iii, 2, 16 : " Fallebat
curas aegraque corda labor," work was lightening our cares and our heavy
hearts.

15 30.   **materials.**   England received, and still receives, from America
many of the raw materials for her manufactures.

15 32.   **curious.**   Interesting.

16 12.   **Roman charity.**   A reference to a story told by Hyginus in his
Fabularum Liber.   Cymon, condemned to death by starvation in prison,
was visited by his daughter Xanthippe, who kept him alive with the milk
from her breast.

16 15.   **fully opened.**   See 3 8, note.   In the course of the debate on restricting the colonies from the Newfoundland fisheries, the general question
of the fisheries was pretty fully discussed, and most of the facts mentioned
in this paragraph were brought out.   Testimony was offered at the bar of
the lords by merchants, fishermen, and others.   See *P. H.*, 381–385,
387–390, 423–430, 433, 437, 438, 459.   See also *A. R.*, 1775, chapter vi.

16 17.   **excite your envy.**   A reference to some of the remarks during
the discussion of the fisheries.   On February 28 a petition was presented
from the inhabitants of Pool, an English fishing town, who said the

restrictions "will not by any means be injurious to commerce, . . . because the foreign markets can be amply supplied by extending the Newfoundland fishery of subjects resident in England." *P. H.*, 382. On March 15 Mr Brooke Watson, a merchant, testified that "the greatest part of the profits arising from the American fishery centres in America" (427); and "that if New England was restrained forever from this fishery, it would be a benefit to Great Britain." 428. Mr. George Davis, a merchant, added "that if this act should pass, he should reap benefit from it; that he has already enlarged his capital, and shall enlarge it more, if the act passes." 429. Molyneux Shuldham, governor of Newfoundland, declared "that if this temporary restraint on the New England fishery was made perpetual, it would be a benefit to Great Britain." 430. Sir Hugh Palliser, formerly a governor of Newfoundland, testified "that whether the restraining of the New England fishery is temporary or perpetual, it will be an advantage to Great Britain." 430.

16 29. **Serpent.** The Hydrus, or Water Serpent, a small constellation within the Antarctic Circle. **Falkland Island.** The Falkland Islands, southeast of South America, were discovered in 1592, but were not regarded as worth occupying till in 1763 the French built Port Louis on East Falkland. Then the Spanish laid claim to the islands; and finally in 1770 and 1771 Spain and England disputed possession. Although many Englishmen thought the islands not worth fighting for, — a fact to which Burke may refer in line 31, — both nations were preparing for war, when in 1771 the Spanish yielded to the English. Later the islands became a place where whalers obtained provisions and water. The *Annual Register*, 1771, chapters i–v, contains a long account of the islands and the trouble with Spain. Cook notes that just a week before Burke's speech, Seth Jenkins, a sailor, testified before the House of Lords that the "limits of the whale fishery extend to Falkland's Island and the coast of Africa." *P. H.*, 423.

17 2. **run the longitude.** Run the course of the meridian, go north or south. While some New Englanders go to Africa, others sail south to Brazil.

17 4. **vexed.** A Latinism founded on similar uses of the Latin *vexare*. Compare, "From the still-vex'd Bermoothes." *Tempest*, act i, scene 2, 229. "As mad as the vex'd sea." *King Lear*, iv, 4, 2.

> When with fierce winds Orion arm'd
> Hath vex'd the Red Sea coast.
>
> *Paradise Lost*, i, 305, 306.

No climate. Compare, "Quae regio in terris nostri non plena laboris?" **What** region of the earth is not full of our toils? Virgil's *Aeneid*, i, 460.

17 8. **hardy.** Bold, adventurous. Compare, "In the last session the corps called *the king's friends* made a hardy attempt, all at once, to alter the right of election itself." *Thoughts on the Cause of the Present Discontents, W.,* I, 496.

17 15. **generous.** High-spirited : originally *high-born* ; then having the qualities which should accompany high birth.

17 25. **well worth fighting for.** This argument had been more than once advanced in Parliament. For example, on January 26 Mr. Hans Stanley had said that "to support the sovereignty was to support the trade of Great Britain ; and if in attempting this arduous task, our commerce should be suspended, our funds should sustain a shock, and the landed property of individuals should experience a diminution, yet all these were evils gentlemen should patiently endure with firmness and magnanimity ; the merchants should forego their own interests for the sake of those permanent advantages which they would undoubtedly reap when the Americans were subdued." *P. H.,* 186.

17 28. **complexions.** Used in the old sense of *temperaments* or *characters*.

17 29. **military art.** Several members of the House who were, or had been, in the army were urging force. On February 2 Colonel Grant had declared that force would overawe the Americans, for "they would never dare to face an English army." *P. H.,* 226. Four days later Captain Harvey had demanded the most firm and vigorous measures. 243. Then on February 27 General Burgoyne had made a fiery speech in favor of force. He said : "It must not be forgot we are contending in the crisis and for the fate of the British Empire. . . . Is there a man in England (I am confident there is not an officer or soldier in the king's service) who does not think the parliamentary rights of Great Britain a cause to fight for, to bleed and die for ? . . . If this [unwillingness to use force] be our wretched state, I agree that the sooner a formal surrender is made, the better ; let Great Britain revert to her primitive insignificancy in the map of the world, and the Congress of Philadelphia be the legislature to dispense the blessings of empire. Let us spare the blood of our subjects, let us spare the treasures of the state ; but let us at the same time confess we are no longer a people." 355-357.

17 30. **wield the thunder.** An allusion to Jove and his thunderbolts. Lord North, it will be remembered, advocated force.

18 5. **temporary.** See 10 30, note.

18 6. **subduing again.** Compare Milton, *Paradise Lost,* i, 648, 649 :

> Who overcomes
> By force, hath overcome but half his foe.

18 10. **without resource.** It had been argued in Parliament that since the Americans now refused to obey, England, even after a war, could be no worse off than at present. Lord North is reported to have said: "If we fail in our attempt of forcing America, we shall still be in the same situation we are in at present." *P. H.*, 262.

18 13. **never be begged.** Compare, "Power and eminence and consideration are things not to be begged; they must be commanded: and they who supplicate for mercy from others can never hope for justice through themselves. What justice they are to obtain, as the alms of an enemy, depends upon his character." *First Letter on a Regicide Peace, W.*, V, 242.

18 15. **impair the object.** See 3 8, note; 30 34; 38 1.

18 21. **British strength.** A little later, 26 12, Burke calls this contest of Englishmen with English an "unnatural contention."

18 22. **foreign enemy.** Throughout the debates on American affairs the fact was constantly urged that France or Spain might take advantage of England, when she was weakened by war with her colonies. For example, on February 2 Captain Luttrell had used this argument (*P. H.*, 231); and February 6 Lord Irnham had brought it up again. 251.

18 26. **break the American spirit.** Members of both houses had argued that it was desirable to break the rebellious spirit of the colonies. On January 20 in the Lords the Earl of Suffolk "insisted strongly that the mother country should never relax till America confessed her supremacy." *P. H.*, 161. On February 6 in the Commons Mr. Hans Stanley urged forcing the colonists to submission. 248. On February 27 Lord North wanted them reduced to "unconditional obedience" (352); and on March 6 Mr. Henry Dundas wished to give them the alternative of starvation or submission. 388.

18 28. **experience.** See 6 15, note.

18 31. **indulgence.** On April 19, 1774, during the debate on the motion to repeal the American Tea Duty Bill, General Burgoyne said: "I look upon America to be our child, which I think we have already spoiled by too much indulgence." *P. H.*, XVII, 1271. Similar expressions may be found in the remarks of Mr. Harris (*ibid.*, 1282) and Mr. Stanley. 1304.

19 8. **temper.** Compare, "The temper of the people amongst whom he presides ought therefore to be the first study of a statesman." *Thoughts on the Cause of the Present Discontents, W.*, I, 436.

19 13. **restive.** Disposed to rest, or stay, unwilling to move forward, balky, obstinate, impatient under restraint.

19 22. **descendants of Englishmen.** In a proposed address to the king, drawn up two years later, Burke says: "Your English subjects in

the colonies, still impressed with the ancient feelings of the people from whom they are derived, cannot live under a government which does not establish freedom as its basis." *W.*, VI, 164.

19 24. **formerly adored.** Burke, in his *Thoughts on the Cause of the Present Discontents,* published in 1770, argued that Englishmen were losing their zeal for liberty and allowing the crown to encroach on their rights.

19 25. **emigrated from you.** During the struggles against the Stuarts in the first half of the seventeenth century.

19 29. **abstract liberty.** Compare, "There are people who have split and anatomized the doctrine of free government, as if it were an abstract question concerning metaphysical liberty and necessity, and not a matter of moral prudence and natural feeling. . . . Civil freedom, Gentlemen, is not, as many have endeavored to persuade you, a thing that lies hid in the depth of abstruse science. It is a blessing and a benefit, not an abstract speculation." *Letter to the Sheriffs of Bristol, W.,* II, 228, 229. (Cook.)

19 31. **sensible.** The primary meaning, *capable of being perceived by the senses.* There is a similar passage in Burke's speech upon his arrival at Bristol the preceding October: "It [liberty] inheres in good and steady government, as in its substance and vital principle." *W.,* II, 87. **every nation.** Compare Goldsmith's *Traveller,* 93–96 :

> Hence every state to one lov'd blessing prone,
> Conforms and models life to that alone.
> Each to the favorite happiness attends,
> And spurns the plan that aims at other ends.

19 34. **great contests.** For example, the contest for Magna Charta.

20 2. **ancient commonwealths.** Rome and the states of Greece.

20 4. **several orders.** For example, the patricians and the plebeians.

20 7. **ablest pens.** Pym, Hampden, Selden, St. John. (Payne.)

20 14. **blind usages.** Usages for which no clear reason can be given.

21 1. **mode of governing.** "The colonies were from the beginning subject to the legislature of Great Britain on principles which they never examined ; and we permitted to them many local privileges, without asking how they agreed with that legislative authority." *Letter to the Sheriffs of Bristol, W.,* II, 231.

21 6. **provincial legislative assemblies.** "The colonies . . . had formed within themselves, either by royal instruction or royal charter, assemblies so exceedingly resembling a Parliament in all their forms, functions, and powers, that it was impossible they should not imbibe some opinion of a similar authority. At . . . first . . . these assemblies . . . were probably not intended for anything more than the municipal corporations within this island. . . . But nothing in its progression can rest on its original plan. . . .

Therefore, as the colonies prospered, . . . it was natural that they should attribute to assemblies so respectable . . . some part of the dignity of the great nations which they represented. No longer tied to by-laws, these assemblies made acts of all sorts and in all cases whatsoever." *Letter to the Sheriffs of Bristol*, W., II, 232.

21 7. **popular.** Used in the primary sense of *belonging directly to the people.* See Bryce's *American Commonwealth*, New York, 1888, I, 562: "Each [early New England settlement] was a religious as well as a civil body politic, gathered round the church as its centre; and the equality which prevailed in the congregation prevailed also in civil affairs, the whole community meeting under a president or moderator to discuss affairs of common interest. Each such settlement was called a town, or township, and was in fact a miniature commonwealth, exercising a practical sovereignty over the property and persons of its members, — for there was as yet no state, and the distant home government scarcely cared to interfere, — but exercising it on thoroughly democratic principles." **merely.** Wholly. Compare, "The one sort we may for distinction call mixedly, and the other merely human." Hooker's *Ecclesiastical Polity*, i, 10. (Payne.)

21 11. **aversion from.** Aversion *to* is now more common.

21 18. **that kind.** Dissenters from the Church of England.

22 3. **refinement on the principle of resistance.** Burke has a fondness for this mode of phrasing. See the next two lines. Compare also the following passages : "The first fruits of that insurrection grafted on insurrection and of that rebellion improving upon rebellion." *Preface to Brissot's Address to his Constituents*, W., V, 85, 86. "They have apostatized from their apostasy." *Fourth Letter on a Regicide Peace*, W., VI, 86.

22 6. **communion.** Union in doctrine and discipline.

22 11. **this spirit was high.** See 19 25, note.

22 15. **establishments.** Churches supported by the state.

22 21. **has a regular establishment.** Is the formally established state church.

22 26. **vast multitude.** See 10 9, note.

22 31. **as broad and general as the air.** Compare *Macbeth*, iii, 4, 23: "As broad and general as the casing air."

23 7. **Gothic.** A word which Burke and other eighteenth-century writers often use in the general sense of *Germanic* or *Teutonic*. Compare, "The whole of the polity and economy of every country in Europe has been derived from the same sources. It was drawn from the old Germanic, or Gothic, custumary." *First Letter on a Regicide Peace*, W., V, 319. The English are not descended from the Goths, properly so called.

23 8. **Poles.** Till the partition of Poland in 1772, the peasants were

serfs attached to the soil. See *A. R.*, 1763, 45: "Each noble Pole . . . is absolute master of life and death on his own estate, all his tenants being in the strictest sense his slaves."

23 15. **law.** Among the papers presented to Parliament in 1766, relating to the disturbances over the Stamp Act, is one written from New York, December 13, 1765, containing the following passages : " The gentlemen of the law, both the judges and the principal practitioners at the bar, are either owners or strongly connected in family interest with the proprietors in general. The gentlemen of the law some years since entered into an association, with intention among other things to assume the direction of government upon them by the influence they had in the assembly, gained by their family connection and by the profession of the law, whereby they are unavoidably in the secrets of many families. Many court their friendship, and all dread their hatred ; by these means, though few of them are members, they rule the house of the assembly in all matters of importance. . . . By this association, united in interest and family connections with the proprietors of the great tracts, a domination of lawyers was formed in this province, which for some years past has been too strong for the executive powers of government." *P. H.*, XVI, 125. Lecky, in chapter xii, discusses the influence, not only of the study of law, but of general education in the colonies. III, 315–317.

23 25. **Blackstone's Commentaries.** Sir William Blackstone was born in 1723 and died in 1780. His *Commentaries on the Laws of England* was published in 1765–1769, and is still the great authority on the subject.

23 26. **General Gage.** Thomas Gage was born in 1721 and died in 1787. His part in the Revolutionary War is pretty well known to every schoolboy. In 1760 he became governor of Montreal. Three years later he was appointed commander-in-chief of the English forces in America. Then in 1774 he was made governor-in-chief and captain-general of Massachusetts. See *D. N. B.*

23 27. **letter on your table.** During the previous session, Parliament, acting on the idea that town-meetings were likely to stir up sedition, passed an act forbidding them in Massachusetts, except by permission of the governor. This act Governor Gage was called upon to enforce. A letter which he wrote from Salem, August 27, 1774, and which Lord North laid before the House January 19, 1775, tells of the result of his attempts : " My former letters have acquainted your lordship that the acts in question had been published here, and people have had leisure to consider means to elude them, in doing which they are very expert. At a town-meeting held in Boston in July, in order to avoid the calling a meeting afterwards, they adjourned themselves to the ninth of August, and adjourned again on that

day to some time in October. I assembled the selectmen in Boston, had the clause read respecting town-meetings, told them I expected their obedience to it, that I should put the act in force, and that they would be answerable for any bad consequences. They replied they had called no meeting, that a former meeting had only adjourned themselves. I laid the affair of adjournments before the new council, and found some of opinion that the clause was thereby clearly evaded, and nearly the whole unwilling to debate upon it, terming it a point of law which ought to be referred to the crown lawyers, whose opinion is to be taken upon it, and by which I must govern myself." *P. H.*, 90, 91. In a letter of September 2, General Gage writes : " With regard to the clause in the new acts relative to town-meetings, so many elusions are discovered under various pretensions of adjournments, electing to vacant offices, people assembling peaceably without notification, upon their own affairs, and withal no penalty, that no persons I have advised with can tell what to do with it ; at a distance they go on as usual, but worse transactions make that matter of little conse quence in the present moment." *P. H.*, 95. See 21 7, note.

24 1. **friend.** Lord Edward Thurlow, who was appointed attorney-general in 1771, and who was a warm supporter of Lord North. He was the first speaker to reply to Burke. **floor.** The benches of the House of Commons are arranged in tiers. The lowest, that on the floor, to the right of the Speaker, is occupied by cabinet members, in which number the attorney-general is included.

24 8. **Abeunt studia in mores.** One's studies (or pursuits) become a part of one's character. Ovid, *Heroides*, xv, 83. Compare Bacon's essay *Of Studies :* " Histories make men wise; poets, witty ; the mathematics, subtle ; natural philosophy, deep ; moral, grave; logic and rhetoric, able to contend. *Abeunt studia in mores.*"

24 25. **winged ministers.** Ships, which are compared to the eagle that carried Jupiter's thunderbolts in its pounces, or talons. The image may have been suggested to Burke by Lord Chatham, who in a speech, January 22, 1770, said of the army : " They [the ministers] have disarmed the imperial bird, the 'ministrum fulminis alitem.' [Horace, *Odes*, iv, 4, 1.] The army is the thunder of the crown. The ministry have tied up the hand which should direct the bolt." *P. H.*, XVI, 750. (Goodrich.)

24 29. **" So far shalt thou go."** Compare *Job*, xxxviii, 11: " Hitherto shalt thou come, but no further ; and here shall thy proud waves be stayed." Payne and Selby think there is a reference to the story of Canute, popularized by Hume about a dozen years before. In order to teach his flatterers a lesson, the king ordered his chair to be set on the seashore while the tide was rising, and then commanded the waves to retire. " But when the sea

still advanced towards him, and began to wash him with its billows, he turned to his courtiers and remarked to them that every creature in the universe was feeble and impotent, and that power resided with one being alone, in whose hands were all the elements of nature ; who could say to the ocean, *Thus far shalt thou go, and no farther ;* and who could level with his nod the most towering piles of human ambition." *History of England,* chapter iii.

24 30. **fret and rage.** This phrase occurs in one of the earliest known bits of Burke's writing, — a familiar letter sent to a schoolmate, Richard Shackleton, in 1745, when Burke was sixteen years old. "Shall I rage, fret, and accuse Providence of injustice?" *C.,* I, 13.

25 1. **Egypt.** Practically under English control since 1883.

25 3. **Crimea.** Under Russian rule since 1783. **Algiers.** In control of the French since 1830.

25 4. **truck.** Barter.

25 5. **huckster.** A verb from the noun *huckster,* a peddler of small wares. *Huckster* is in turn from the old verb *huck,* to haggle in trading.

25 16. **first mover.** Burke must have had in mind the *primum mobile* of the Ptolemaic astronomy. According to this system the heavenly bodies were set in a series of spheres revolving about the earth as a common centre. The outermost sphere, called the *primum mobile,* or "first moved," communicated its motion to the inner spheres.

25 18. **grown with the growth.** Compare Pope's *Essay on Man,* ii, 136: "Grows with his growth and strengthens with his strength."

26 2. **with all its imperfections.** Compare *Hamlet,* i, 5, 78, 79:

> But sent to my account
> With all my imperfections on my head.

26 7. **a little stability.** See 4 18, note.

26 12. **unnatural contention.** See 18 21.

26 15. **not been.** The Second Edition reads "been not," which later editors have agreed in changing.

26 17. **popular part.** The reference is to the representative assemblies which were convoked by the governors, who were in turn nominated by the crown.

26 25. **none but an obedient assembly.** The Virginia Assembly was dissolved by Governor Dunmore in May, 1774, because on receiving news of the closing of the port of Boston, this body had passed resolutions denying the authority of Parliament. The result, to which Burke refers a few lines below, is told by Governor Dunmore in a letter sent from Williamsburg, December 24, 1774, and laid before the House February 15, 1775.

" As to the power of government which your lordship . . . directs should be exerted to counteract the dangerous measures pursuing here, I can assure your lordship that it is entirely disregarded, if not wholly overturned. There is not a justice of peace in Virginia that acts, except as a committee man [under direction of the local committees organized to carry out the non-importation and non-exportation agreements of the Continental Congress]. The abolishing the courts of justice was the first step taken, in which the men of fortune joined equally with the lowest and meanest. The general court of judicature of the colony is much in the same predicament; for though there are at least a majority of his Majesty's council who, with myself, are the judges of that court, that would steadily perform their duty, yet the lawyers have absolutely refused to attend, nor indeed would the people allow them to attend, or evidences to appear. . . . Independent companies, etc., so universally supported, who have set themselves up superior to all other authority, under the auspices of their Congress, the laws of which they talk of in a style of respect, and treat with marks of reverence which they never bestowed on their legal government or the laws proceeding from it, — I can assure your lordship that I have discovered no instance where the interposition of government, in the feeble state to which it is reduced, could serve any other purpose than to suffer the disgrace of a disappointment, and thereby afford matter of great exultation to its enemies, and increase their influence over the minds of the people." *P. H.*, 314, 315.

26 26. **humors.** An allusion to the old theory that the body contained various humors, or fluids, which might become diseased, and, finding no vent in natural channels, break out in boils or other eruptions.

26 34. **Lord Dunmore.** John Murray, fourth Earl of Dunmore: born, 1732; died, 1809. In 1770 he was appointed governor of New York, and later of Virginia. In 1775 the feeling against him ran so high that he had to flee for refuge to a man-of-war. For a time he carried on hostilities against the colony, burning the important town of Norfolk. See *D. N. B.*

27 3. **Obedience.** See 4 8, note. Compare also, " Whether the immediate and instrumental cause of the law be a single person or many, the remote and efficient cause is the consent of the people, either actual or implied; and such consent is absolutely essential to its validity." *Tract on the Popery Laws*, *W.*, VI, 320. This suggests a sentence in the *Declaration of Independence*, "To secure these rights, governments are instituted among men, deriving their just powers from the consent of the governed."

27 18. **abrogated.** The reference is to an act passed May 11, 1774, entitled " An Act for the better regulating the government of the province of the Massachusetts Bay in New England." See 58 23. By this act,

which changed the charter of the province, the council, or upper chamber
of the legislature, hitherto elected by the assembly, or lower chamber
directly representative of the people, was appointed by the crown; the
judges and magistrates of all kinds, including sheriffs, were appointed by
the royal governor, who could remove at pleasure; jurymen, instead of
being chosen by popular election, were summoned by the sheriffs; and no
town-meetings could be held without permission of the governor. See
Lecky, III, 431; *P. H.*, XVII, 1192–1199, 1277–1289, 1297–1316, 1321–
1325; *A. R.*, 1774, 69–72.

27 19. **confident.** In the parliamentary debates over the changes in
the charter of Massachusetts the opinion was more than once expressed
that this act would settle the troubles. On March 28, 1774, Lord North
said he thought the bill would "effectually purge" the constitution of
Massachusetts of its crudities, and give strength and spirit to the civil
magistracy and the executive. *P. H.*, XVII, 1193. On the same day Lord
George Germain declared: "I make no doubt but by a manly and steady
perseverance things may be restored from a state of anarchy and confusion
to peace, quietude, and a due obedience to the laws of this country." *Ibid.*,
1196. On April 19 Mr. Cornwall said: "If you persist in the measures
you have begun with, I think there is not a doubt of your succeeding, and
of becoming, if I may use the word, victorious." *Ibid.*, 1215. On the same
day Lord North again said: "Let us conduct ourselves with firmness and
resolution throughout the whole of these measures, and there is not the
least doubt but peace and quietude will soon be restored." *Ibid.*, 1273.

27 22. **Anarchy is found tolerable.** General Gage, in a letter from
Boston, November 2, 1774, said that the province was "without courts of
justice or legislature"; and also that the edicts of the provincial Congress
were "implicitly obeyed throughout the country." *P. H.*, 105. The account
in the *Annual Register* for 1775, 17, is as follows: "The old constitution
being taken away by act of Parliament, and the new one being rejected by
the people, an end was put to all forms of law and government in the
province of Massachusetts Bay, and the people were reduced to that state
of anarchy in which mankind are supposed to have existed in the earliest
ages. The degree of order, however, which by the general concurrence of
the people was preserved in this state of anarchy will forever excite the
astonishment of mankind, and continue among the strongest proofs of the
efficacy of long-established habits and of a constant submission to laws.
Excepting the general opposition to the new government, and excesses
arising from it, in the outrages offered to particular persons who were upon
that account obnoxious to the people, no other very considerable marks
appeared of the cessation of law or of government."

28 5. **in order to prove.** Compare 19 22, note; 31 17; also, " The feel-ings of the colonies were formerly the feelings of Great Britain. Theirs were formerly the feelings of Mr. Hampden, when called upon for the payment of twenty shillings. Would twenty shillings have ruined Mr. Hampden's fortune? No! but the payment of half twenty shillings on the principle it was demanded would have made him a slave." *Speech on American Taxation, W.,* II, 17. " As it will be impossible long to resist the powerful and equitable arguments in favor of the freedom of these unhappy people that are to be drawn from the principle of our own liberty, attempts will be made, attempts have been made, to ridicule and to argue away this principle, and to inculcate into the minds of your people other maxims of government and other grounds of obedience than those which have prevailed at and since the glorious Revolution." *Address to the King, W.,* VI, 177, 178.

28 19. **but three ways.** Later in the speech Burke touches on a fourth plan, that of giving the colonies representation. See 53 6–12. This method he discusses at some length in the *Present State of the Nation, W.,* I, 372–376.

28 26. **giving up the colonies.** This plan, as Cook notes, was proposed in 1774 by Dr. Josiah Tucker, Dean of Gloucester, in a publication, *Four Tracts on Political and Commercial Subjects.* In the last paper in the vol-ume, entitled *The True Interest of Great Britain set forth in regard to the Colonies, and the only Means of living in Peace and Harmony with them,* he urged that the colonies be allowed to separate from England. They were, he argued, of no advantage to the mother country, except for trade. If Eng-land offered America the best markets, England would get the trade, even were America independent. If England failed to offer the best markets, she would inevitably lose the trade, and she might at the same time be at a heavy loss in trying to retain the colonies. These tracts and others by Dean Tucker — including a reply to this very speech by Burke — were often reprinted in England and America. See Lecky, III, 421–424.

29 25. **Appalachian Mountains.** See Bancroft, III, 467 : " An intrepid population, heedless of proclamations, was pouring westward through all the gates of the Alleghanies ; seating themselves on the New River and the Greenbrier, on the branches of the Monongahela, or even making their way to the Mississippi." (Cook.)

29 34. **comptrollers.** The common spelling or controller, an officer who keeps a counter roll, or duplicate account, by which to control, or supervise, the accounts of another officer, usually a treasurer.

30 4. **" Increase and multiply."** Compare *Genesis,* i, 28 : " God said unto them, ' Be fruitful and multiply.' " *Paradise Lost,* x, 729, 730 :

O voice once heard
Delightfully, " Increase and multiply."

30 6. **given to the children of men.** Compare *Psalms*, cxv, 16: " The earth hath he given to the children of men." Also, " God has given the earth to the children of men." *Two Letters to Gentlemen in Bristol, W.,* II, 260.

30 21. **marine enterprises.** See 3 8, note ; 16 17, note.

30 26. **we must gain.** Compare, " It is hard to persuade us that everything which is *got* by another is not *taken* from ourselves. But it is fit that we should get the better of these suggestions, which come from what is not the best and soundest part of our nature." *Two Letters to Gentlemen in Bristol, W.,* II, 260.

30 34. **unserviceable.** See 3 8, note ; 38 1.

31 2. **exploded.** From *ex* and *plaudere*, to clap the hands. The word was sometimes applied to a play which was hooted off the stage, and it is here used in a similar sense. Compare, " If the affections and opinions of mankind be not exploded as principles of connection, I conceive it would be happy for us if they [the Americans] were taught to believe that there was even a formed American party in England." *Letter to the Sheriffs of Bristol, W.,* II, 215.

31 9. **Spoliatis arma supersunt.** Freely translated, The plundered yet have a resource in arms. From Juvenal, *Satires*, viii, 124.

31 12. **this fierce people.** See Introduction, xiii.

31 16. **your speech.** Compare *Matthew*, xxvi, 73: " Thy speech bewrayeth thee."

31 17. **unfittest person.** See 19 22, note ; 28 5, note.

31 27. **books of curious science.** Law books. Compare *Acts*, xix, 19: " Many of them also which used curious arts brought their books together and burned them."

31 33. **chargeable.** Costly.

31 34. **obedience.** Compare, " Fierce licentiousness begets violent restraints. The military arm is the sole reliance ; and then, call your constitution what you please, it is the sword that governs. The civil power, like every other that calls in the aid of an ally stronger than itself, perishes by the assistance it receives." *Thoughts on the Cause of the Present Discontents, W.,* I, 484. " That the establishment of such a [military] power in America will utterly ruin our finances — though its certain effect — is the smallest part of our concern. It will become an apt, powerful, and certain engine for the destruction of our freedom here. Great bodies of armed men, trained to a contempt of popular assemblies representative of an English people, — kept up for the purpose of exacting impositions

without their consent, and maintained by that exaction, — instruments in subverting, without any process of law, great ancient establishments and respected forms of governments, — set free from, and therefore above, the ordinary English tribunals of the country where they serve, — these men cannot so transform themselves merely by crossing the sea, as to behold with love and reverence, and submit with profound obedience to, the very same things in Great Britain which in America they had been taught to despise, and had been accustomed to awe and humble." *Address to the King*, W., VI, 176, 177.

32 4. **advocates and panegyrists.** For example, Dr. Johnson, in his *Taxation No Tyranny*, published not long before this speech was delivered, had said : " It has been proposed that the slaves should be set free, an act which surely the lovers of liberty cannot but commend. If they are furnished with firearms for defence and utensils for husbandry, and settled in some simple form of government within the country, they may be more grateful and honest than their masters " Johnson's *Works*, London, 1820, VIII, 201, 202. (Cook.)

32 7. **would not always be accepted.** In November, 1775, Governor Dunmore of Virginia proclaimed an emancipation of the slaves and summoned them to his standard. Comparatively few, however, joined him. The account may be found in most American histories ; for example, Bancroft, IV, 318.

32 14. **other people.** " See Aristophanes, *Ranae*, 27, from which it appears that the slaves who had distinguished themselves at the battle of Arginusae were presented with their freedom. Plutarch says that Cleomenes armed two thousand Helots to oppose the Macedonian Leucaspedae, in his war with that people and the Achaeans. According to Pausanias the Helots were present at the battle of Marathon. Among the Romans, as Virgil (*Aeneid*, ix, 547) tells us, it was highly criminal for slaves to enter the army of their masters ; but in the Hannibalian war, after the battle of Cannae, eight thousand of them were armed, and by their valor in subsequent actions earned their liberty. See Livy, Book xxiv." (Payne.)

32 21. **their refusal.** During the years preceding the Revolution, several of the colonies attempted to restrict the slave trade, but the English government interfered, and this interference was one cause of grievance to the Americans. In 1761 Virginia proposed to abandon the trade (Bancroft, II, 549), but in behalf of English merchants, the home government refused to allow restrictions. In the same year South Carolina made a similar proposal (*ibid.*, 550), which met with similar opposition. In 1772 Virginia again protested (III, 411); and one of Lord Dunmore's last acts was to veto a bill to check the trade by a heavy duty on slaves. IV, 202.

When he issued his proclamation of freedom, "the Virginians," says Ban croft (IV, 318), "could plead and did plead that 'their assemblies had repeatedly attempted to prevent the horrid traffic in slaves, and had been frustrated by the cruelty and covetousness of English merchants, who had prevailed on the king to repeal their merciful acts.'"

32 26. **Guinea captain.** English captain of a ship engaged in the Guinea trade.

32 33. **"Ye gods."** From *Martinus Scriblerus, of the Art of Sinking in Poetry*, written by Pope, Swift, and Arbuthnot, — chiefly the last mentioned; published in 1741. The two lines are in the first part of chapter xi, as an example of hyperbole. Pope's *Works*, 1776, IV, 169.

33 7. **late.** Recent.

33 11. **criminal.** The idea of punishing the colonists as criminals was repeatedly urged by the adherents of the ministry. On March 23, 1774, during the debate on the Boston Port Bill, Mr. Rose Fuller said : " We all agree that the Bostonians ought to be punished." *P. H.*, XVII, 1176. On the same day Mr. Van said he agreed to the flagitiousness of the offence of the Americans, and therefore was of opinion that the town of Boston ought to be knocked about their ears and destroyed. "*Delenda est Carthago*," said he, " I am of opinion you will never meet with proper obedience to the laws of this country until you have destroyed that nest of locusts." *Ibid.*, 1178. On April 15 of the same year Mr. Van advocated burning the forests and leaving the country open, so that the Americans might be deprived of protection. *Ibid.*, 1210. On March 6, 1775, Mr. Henry Dundas declared the " grand penal bill " just, because it was " provoked by the most criminal disobedience : it was merciful, because that disobedience would have justified the severest military execution." *P. H.*, XVIII, 387. On March 16, during a debate in the Lords on the same bill, the Duke of Grafton said the measure was "founded on the principle of retaliation and punishment." *Ibid.*, 451.

33 23. **indictment against a whole people.** Compare, "I am not for a total indemnity, nor a general punishment. And first, the body and mass of the people never ought to be treated as criminal. They may become an object of more or less constant watchfulness and suspicion, as their preservation may best require, but they can never become an object of punishment. This is one of the few fundamental and unalterable principles of politics." *On the Policy of the Allies*, 1793, *W.*, IV, 462.

33 25. **Sir Edward Coke.** An eminent lawyer: born, 1552; died, 1634. In 1603, while serving as attorney-general, he conducted the trial of Sir Walter Ralegh for treason. On this occasion, according to the *D. N. B.*, XI, 230, 231, " he exhibited a spirit of rancor, descending even to brutality,

for which no one has attempted a defence, his biographers one and all agreeing that his conduct toward Ralegh was simply infamous. ' Thy Machiavelian and devilish policy,' ' thou hast a Spanish heart, and thyself art a spider of hell,' ' I will now make it appear to the world that there never lived a viler viper upon the face of the earth than thou,' — these are some of the flowers of his speech. ' The extreme weakness of the evidence,' says Sir James Stephen, ' was made up for by the rancorous ferocity of Coke, who reviled and insulted Ralegh in a manner never imitated, so far as I know, before or since in any English court of justice, except perhaps in those in which Jeffreys presided.' "

33 26. **Sir Walter Ralegh.** Explorer, author, statesman : born, 1552 ; executed, 1618. He was accused of complicity in the plots against James the First.

33 29. **very same title.** Members of the colonial assemblies, like members of Parliament, were chosen by popular vote.

34 2. **one common head.** Compare, " The Parliament of Great Britain sits at the head of her extensive empire in two capacities : one as the local legislature of this island, providing for all things at home, immediately and by no other instrument than the executive power ; the other, and I think her nobler capacity, is what I call her *imperial character*, in which, as from the throne of heaven, she superintends all the several inferior legislatures, and guides and controls them all without annihilating any." *Speech on American Taxation, W.,* II, 75.

34 8. **nice.** " Apprehending slight differences or delicate distinctions."

34 12. **ex vi termini.** From the force of the term, or meaning of the word. The Roman *privilegium* was a law giving an individual some special privilege, or laying him under some special restriction.

34 20. **[that].** This word, though in the Second Edition, is clearly unnecessary, and is therefore bracketed. (Cook.)

34 31. **judge in my own cause.** Compare, " One of the first motives to civil society, and which becomes one of its fundamental rules, is *that no man should be judge in his own cause.* By this each person has at once divested himself of the first fundamental right of uncovenanted man, that is, to judge for himself and to assert his own cause." *Reflections on the Revolution in France, W.,* III, 309, 310. On February 6, 1775, during a debate in the Commons over an address to the king concerning the disturbances in America, Governor Johnstone said : " Judge Hobert says, ' If an act of Parliament was made constituting a man a judge in his own cause, it would be void by the law of nature.' Yet such is the precise situation in which we contend we ought to be placed respecting the Americans, and for the

denial of which we are ready to condemn our fellow subjects to all the tortures enacted by the laws of treason." *P. H.*, 254.

35 4. **against the superior.** Compare, " In all disputes between them [the people] and their rulers, the presumption is at least upon a par in favor of the people. Experience may perhaps justify me in going further. When popular discontents have been very prevalent, it may well be affirmed and supported that there has been generally something found amiss in the constitution or in the conduct of government." *Thoughts on the Cause of the Present Discontents, W.*, I, 440. " We are convinced that the disorders of the people in the present time and in the present place are owing to the usual and natural cause of such disorders at all times and in all places where such have prevailed, — the misconduct of government." *Address to the King, W.*, VI, 163.

35 6. **abstract right.** See 7 14, note.

35 10. **injustice.** An allusion to the maxim, *Summum jus, summa injuria*, The extreme of the law is the extreme of injustice, Cicero, *De Officiis*, i, 10. Compare, " When confidence is once restored, the odious and suspicious *summum jus* will perish of course." *Speech on American Taxation, W.*, II, 71.

35 12. **civil litigant.** A litigant in a suit in which legal rights but not crimes are involved. The first question was whether England had a right to tax the colonies; the second, whether America was criminal in resisting.

35 22. **those very persons.** The majority in Parliament.

35 23. **declaring a rebellion.** On February 9, 1775, both Houses joined in an address to the king containing the following passage: " We find that a part of your Majesty's subjects in the province of the Massachusetts Bay have proceeded so far to resist the authority of the supreme legislature that a rebellion at this time actually exists within the said province." *P. H.*, 297. Against this address the minority of the Lords offered a protest which seems to express Burke's view: " No legal grounds were laid in argument or in fact to show that a rebellion, properly so called, did exist in Massachusetts Bay when the papers of the latest date, and from whence alone we derive our information, were written. The overt acts to which the species of treason affirmed in the address ought to be applied were not established, nor were any offenders marked out. But a general mass of the acts of turbulence, said to be done at various times and places, were all thrown together to make out one general constructive treason. Neither was there any sort of proof of the continuance of any unlawful force from whence we could infer that a rebellion does now exist. And we are the more cautious of pronouncing any part of his Majesty's dominion to be in rebellion, because the cases of constructive treason under that branch of

the twenty-fifth of Edward the Third which describes the crime of rebellion have been already so far extended by the judges, and the distinctions thereupon so nice and subtle, that no prudent man ought to declare any single person in that situation without the clearest evidence of uncontrovertible overt acts to warrant such a declaration. Much less ought so high an authority as both Houses of Parliament to denounce so severe a judgment against a considerable part of his Majesty's subjects, by which his forces may think themselves justified in commencing a war without any further order or commission." *P. H.*, 294, 295.

35 24. **formerly addressed.** On February 13, 1769, a joint address was presented to the king, pledging support in any measures needful to maintain authority in Massachusetts. The address continues: "As . . . nothing can be more immediately necessary . . . than to proceed in the most speedy and effectual manner for bringing to condign punishment the chief authors and instigators of the late disorders, we most humbly beseech your Majesty . . . to direct your Majesty's governor of Massachusetts Bay to take the most effectual methods for procuring the fullest information that can be obtained touching all treasons, or misprision of treason, committed within this government since the 30th day of December last, . . . together with the names of the persons who were most active in the commission of such offences, . . . in order that your Majesty may issue a special commission for inquiring of, hearing and determining the said offences within this realm, pursuant to the provisions of the statute of the thirty-fifth year of the reign of King Henry the Eighth." *P. H.*, XVI, 479, 480. In the *Letter to the Sheriffs of Bristol*, 1777, *W.*, II, 192, Burke explains the practical operation of the act referred to in the address: "It is necessary, Gentlemen, to apprise you that there is an act, made so long ago as in the reign of Henry the Eighth, before the existence or thought of any English colonies in America, for the trial in this kingdom of treasons committed out of the realm. In the year 1769 Parliament thought proper to acquaint the crown with their construction of that act in a formal address, wherein they entreated his Majesty to cause persons charged with high treason in America to be brought into this kingdom for trial. By this act of Henry the Eighth, so construed and so applied, almost all that is substantial and beneficial in a trial by jury is taken away from the subject in the colonies. This is, however, saying too little ; for to try a man under that act is, in effect, to condemn him unheard. A person is brought hither in the dungeon of a ship's hold ; thence he is vomited into a dungeon on land, loaded with irons, unfurnished with money, unsupported by friends, three thousand miles from all means of calling upon or confronting evidence, where no one local circumstance that tends to detect perjury can

possibly be judged of; — such a person may be executed according to form, but he can never be tried according to justice." See 59 30–34. The act in question was passed during the session of 1543–1544.

35 34. **juridical.** See 7 14, note.

36 2. **menaces.** During the previous decade Parliament in addresses to the king had made many direct and indirect threats against the colonies. On January 14, 1766, at the time of the agitations over the Stamp Act, the Lords addressed the king, saying : " We will exert our utmost endeavors to assert and support your Majesty's dignity and honor and the legislative authority of this kingdom over its colonies." *P. H.*, XVI, 94. On November 8, 1768, at the opening of Parliament the Lords, in an address echoed by the Commons, declared : " We most unfeignedly give your Majesty the strongest assurances that we shall ever zealously concur in support of such just and necessary measures as may best enable your Majesty to repress that daring spirit of disobedience, and to enforce a due submission to the laws; always considering that it is one of our most essential duties to maintain inviolate the supreme authority of the legislature of Great Britain over every part of the dominions of your Majesty's crown." *Ibid.*, 471. For the next menace, that of February 13, 1769, see 35 24, note. On January 9, 1770, the Lords and Commons, in addresses practically the same in sentiment, said : " We shall be ready to give every assistance in our power . . . for discountenancing those unwarrantable measures practiced in some of your Majesty's colonies, which appear calculated to destroy the commercial connection between them and the mother country." *Ibid.*, 667. On November 13 of the same year both Houses declared : " We will neglect no means of . . . providing for the protection of your Majesty's good subjects there [in the colonies] from every degree of violence and oppression." *Ibid.*, 1080. On November 30, 1774, the Lords expressed their detestation of the disobedience to the laws in Massachusetts, and promised cheerful coöperation in all efforts to suppress it (XVIII, 39); and on December 5 the Commons made the king even stronger assurances of support. *Ibid.*, 46. For the last threat, that of February 9, 1775, see 8 18, note.

36 4. **penal laws.** For a list of laws which Burke regarded as penal and wished to suspend, see 58 1–24. The first, " An act for granting certain duties," passed in 1767, provided for a duty on glass, paper, red and white lead, painters' colors, and tea. *P. H.*, XVI, 375, 376; also *Statutes at Large*, chapter 46 of 7 George the Third. All the duties except those on tea were repealed in 1769, and thus the act is often known as the Tea Duty Bill. The second, " An act to discontinue," passed March, 1774, provided for the closing of the port of Boston, and is known as the Boston Port Bill. *P. H.*, XVII, 1164; also *Statutes at Large*, chapter 19 of 14

George the Third. The third, "An act for the impartial administration of justice," passed May, 1774, provided that if any person in Massachusetts were indicted for murder or any other capital offence, and if it should appear to the governor that the incriminated act was committed in aiding the magistrates to suppress tumult and riot, and also that a fair trial could not be had in the provinces, the prisoner should be sent for trial to any other colony or to Great Britain. *P. H.,* XVII, 1200; also *Statutes at Large,* chapter 39 of 14 George the Third. The fourth, "An act for the better regulating the government," is explained in 27 18, note. To this last may be added two or three other acts, some of them merely temporary in effect. In 1765 a bill had been passed, commonly called the American Mutiny Act, requiring the colonists to supply the English troops with some of the necessaries of life. On the refusal of New York to comply, a bill was passed temporarily suspending the Assembly. *P. H.,* XVI, 331; also *Statutes at Large,* chapter 59 of 7 George the Third. See Introduction, xv–xix.

36 6. **a force.** During a debate on the navy estimate in the Commons on December 12, 1774, it was stated that nineteen vessels containing 2835 seamen were on duty along the American coast. *P. H.,* 54. On February 15, 1775, in answer to a message from the king, the Commons took up a bill to increase the army, so that there might be about ten thousand men in Boston. *P. H.,* 316.

36 9. **confident hopes.** See 27 19, note.

36 11. **correctly.** Precisely.

36 22. **colonies complain.** See the resolution passed by the American Congress, October 14, 1774: "*Resolved,* That the foundation of English liberty and all free government is a right of the people to participate in their legislative council : and as the English colonists are not represented, and from their local and other circumstances cannot properly be represented, in the British Parliament, they are entitled to a free and exclusive power of legislation in their several provincial legislatures, where their right of representation can alone be preserved, in all cases of taxation and internal polity, subject only to the negative of their sovereign in such manner as has been heretofore used and accustomed." *Journals of Congress,* I, 20.

36 34. **startle.** Now used transitively. Compare Addison's *Cato,* iii, 2, 80, 81 :

> My frightened thoughts run back,
> And startle into madness at the sound.

37 1. **less than nothing.** Compare *Isaiah,* xl, 17 : " All nations before him are as nothing; and they are counted to him less than nothing, and vanity." Also, " In matters of state a constitutional competence to act is

in many cases the smallest part of the question." *First Letter on a Regicide Peace, W.,* V, 283.

37 4. **profound subject.** For a decade the question of the legal right of Parliament to tax the colonies had been debated. Whenever American affairs had been discussed in Parliament, and whenever it was possible to interject remarks on America into the discussion of other subjects, this question had appeared in one form or another. The pages of the *Parliamentary History* and of various contemporary accounts of the proceedings are filled with arguments on the subject ; the periodicals on both sides of the water gave much space to it, and both England and America were flooded with pamphlets on it. Of these last, Dr. Johnson's *Taxation No Tyranny* is a sample. One of the best summaries of the whole discussion is to be found in the *Annual Register* for 1766, reprinted in *P. H.,* XVI, 193–206. This summary shows that the two questions which Burke mentions, lines 6–13, were the ones most often urged. On the one side it was argued that by natural and inalienable right no man could "be taxed but by himself or by his representative." XVI, 195. This argument was presented at considerable length by Mr. Wilkes, February 6, 1775. XVIII, 234–240. On the other hand, it was urged that the very existence of government and the supremacy of Parliament implied the right to tax. XVIII, 241. Each side tried to support its contention (see lines 13–16) by the authority of great lawyers or students of government. "As to the right of taxation, the gentlemen who opposed it produced many learned authorities from Locke, Selden, Harrington, and Puffendorf." *P. H.,* XVI, 194. Burke himself seems to have been of opinion that Parliament had a technical right which it was foolish to exercise. "Mr. Burke observed . . . that we had an undoubted right to tax them [the Americans], but that the expediency of putting that right in execution should be very evident before anything of that sort passed." Debate of March 14, 1769, *P. H.,* XVI, 605. See Introduction, xvi.

37 19. **Serbonian bog.** From *Paradise Lost,* ii, 592–594. The reference is to Lake Serbonis, near the mouth of the Nile.

37 26. **a lawyer tells me.** See 7 14, note.

38 2. **loss of my suit.** Compare 3 8, note ; 18 15 ; also, "It would have been a poor compensation that we had triumphed in a dispute, whilst we lost an empire." *Letter to the Sheriffs of Bristol, W.,* II, 227.

38 5. **unity of spirit.** Compare *I Corinthians,* xii, 4 : "Now there are diversities of gifts, but the same spirit." *Ephesians,* iv, 3 : "Endeavoring to keep the unity of the spirit in the bond of peace."

38 9. **abjured all the rights of citizens.** Dr. Johnson says in *Taxation No Tyranny :* "The Americans have voluntarily resigned the power

of voting, to live in distant and separate governments; and what they have voluntarily quitted, they have no right to claim." *Works*, VIII, 183.

38 21. interest in the Constitution. Compare, "It passes my comprehension in what manner it is that men can be reconciled to the *practical* merits of a constitution . . . by being *practically* excluded from any of its advantages." *Second Letter on the Catholic Question, W.*, VI, 382.

38 27. understood principle. As an act for raising revenue, not controlling trade.

39 3. American financiers. Men who expect much actual revenue from America.

39 4. exquisite. Curious, careful, as in "Over-exquisite to cast the fashion of uncertain evils." *Comus*, 359.

39 9. further views. This argument was common from the beginning of the discussion ten years before. Burke clearly alludes to several of the more recent expressions of it. On April 19, 1774, during a debate on a motion to repeal the Tea Duty Act, Mr. Rice said: "Whenever we have made the least concession, they have always required more; they will think that we acknowledge that we have no right, if we should repeal this law. . . . I am greatly afraid that if you give up this, you will be required to give up much more." *P. H.*, XVII, 1211, 1212. On the same day Mr. Solicitor-General Wedderburn argued: "If you give up this tax, it is not here that you must stop; you will be required to give up much more, nay, to give up all." *Ibid.*, 1270. In a debate in the Lords, January 20, 1775, on Lord Chatham's motion to withdraw the troops from Boston, Lord Lyttelton declared that if Great Britain should give way from mistaken motives of present advantages in trade, such a concession would inevitably defeat its own object; for it was plain that the Navigation Act and all other regulatory acts, which formed the great basis on which those advantages rested, and the true interests of both countries depended, would fall a victim to the interested and ambitious views of America. Every concession would produce a new demand, and in the end bring about that state of traitorous independency at which America was aiming. XVIII, 163. On January 23, while the Commons were considering some petitions for conciliation from merchants of London and Bristol, Lord Stanley insisted that if England gave way, the Americans would desire a repeal of the Navigation Act and every other act on the statute book that in the least degree affected them. *Ibid.*, 177. On March 6, during the argument on Lord North's "grand penal bill," Mr. Rice again said the Americans were aiming at independence, and intended to throw off the commercial restrictions as well as the taxes. On this latter point he was as much inclined to relax as any other member, if he could be sure that such relaxation would not be introductory to a further and worse opposition on their part, 389. To this last speech Burke directly refers in lines 14, 15. See 41 12, note.

39 10. **trade laws.** There had been many laws, some of them called Navigation Acts, passed for restricting the trade of the provinces. By the terms of one act, all colonial exports to England were to be shipped only in American or English vessels; by a second, colonial exports were to go only to England or English colonies; by a third, the colonies could not export hats; and by a fourth, they were forbidden to erect mills for rolling iron or furnaces for making steel. These are but a few of the many harassing regulations laid on the colonies.

39 14. **gentleman.** Mr. Rice. See 39 9, note.

39 23. **noble lord.** See 8 4, note.

39 24. **futile and useless.** The speech in which Lord North made the remarks here attributed to him does not appear in the reports of the debates of 1774 or 1775. On March 5, 1770, during a discussion of the Tea Duty Bill, North argued that American agreements not to buy British goods must speedily be broken, because the colonists could buy more cheaply in England than anywhere else. *P. H.*, XVI, 855.

40 12. **the pamphlet.** By Dr. Tucker. See 28 26, note.

40 14. **idolizing.** Compare, "Among regulations that which stood first in reputation was his [George Grenville's] idol: I mean the Act of Navigation. He has often professed it to be so." *Speech on American Taxation, W.*, II, 38.

40 31. **not a shadow of evidence.** An assertion which Burke could hardly have supported. For a century the Americans had been complaining of the trade laws, as any colonial history will show. For example, when in 1733 Parliament had proposed that after the northern colonies had sold their fish, lumber, and provisions in the West Indies, a return cargo of molasses, sugar, or rum from any but the British West India islands should be subject to a duty, Rhode Island strongly remonstrated, and the New York merchants declared: "The bill is divesting them [the merchants] of their rights as the king's natural-born subjects and Englishmen, in levying subsidies on them against their consent, when they are annexed to no county in Britain, have no representation in Parliament, nor are any part of the legislature of this kingdom. It will be drawn into a precedent hereafter." Bancroft, II, 244.

41 12. **colonies will go further.** See 39 9, note. Compare also, "But still it sticks in our throats, if we go so far, the Americans will go farther. We do not know that. We ought from experience rather to presume the contrary. Do we not know for certain that the Americans are going on as fast as possible, whilst we refuse to gratify them? Can they do more, or can

they do worse, if we yield this point? I think this concession will rather fix a turnpike to prevent their further progress." *Speech on American Taxation, W.*, II, 29. (Cook.)

42 5. **Austrian family.** Emperor Charles the Fifth of Austria inherited the throne of Spain from his mother. This dynasty continued till 1700.

42 8. **Philip the Second.** A son of Charles the Fifth: born in 1527; married Queen Mary of England in 1554; came to the throne of Spain in 1556; fitted out the Spanish Armada in 1588; and died in 1598. He was far from a "perfect standard," for he was a dull, bigoted man. **issue of their affairs.** In 1775 Spain, though relatively stronger than to-day, had already lost much of her ancient power.

42 13. **English Constitution.** This is not, like the Constitution of the United States, a definite document; the phrase refers to the body of traditions, customs, precedents, laws, and institutions, and to the general spirit of the English government.

42 16. **Ireland, Wales, Chester and Durham.** These cases had often been cited in the parliamentary debates. See *P. H.*, XVI, 195–198; XVIII, 235.

42 17. **English conquest.** By Henry the Second, in 1172. For an account of the conquest, see Green, I, 175–178.

42 18. **no Parliament.** Before the conquest Ireland was governed by a number of independent chiefs, each at the head of a *sept*, corresponding to a Scottish clan.

42 22. **such as England then enjoyed.** "The great councils of barons and prelates which he [Henry the Second] summoned year by year." Green, I, 167.

42 28. **Magna Charta.** The Great Charter of rights which the barons forced King John to sign in 1215. It provides among other things that "No scutage or aid . . . shall be imposed in our realm save by the common council of the realm." Green, I, 246.

42 34. **all Ireland.** English laws and liberties were enjoyed by English settlers only who lived within a certain district called the "Pale." It was not until the time of James the First that the privileges of the Pale were extended to the whole country. See Green, I, 514–517.

43 3. **Sir John Davies.** Born, 1569; speaker of the first Irish House of Commons; died in 1626. He published a number of poems, and in 1612 a book called *Discovery of the true Causes why Ireland was never entirely Subdued nor brought under Obedience of the Crown of England until the Beginning of his Majesty's happy Reign.*

43 7. **military government.** A reference to the attempts of the Earl of Essex and Lord Mountjoy to put down rebellions at the close of the sixteenth century. Green. II, 496, 497.

43 9. **civility.** Civilization.

43 13. **changed the people.** A considerable part of the country was settled by the English and Scotch at the Plantation of Ulster, in 1610. Green, III, 154.

43 14. **altered the religion.** From the Church of Rome to the Church of England.

43 16. **deposed kings.** Charles the First in 1649 and James the Second in 1688. **restored them.** Charles the Second was restored in 1660. **altered the succession.** In 1714, from the House of Stuart to the House of Hanover.

43 19. **usurpation.** The protectorate of Cromwell, 1649-1660.

43 20. **glorious Revolution.** Burke calls the Revolution of 1688 *glorious* because it was a triumph of the Whig principles, in which he believed. His views are very fully set forth in his *Appeal from the New to the Old Whigs*. See 28 5, note.

43 22. **disgrace and a burden.** For centuries the government of Ireland was one of the most serious questions with which England had to deal.

43 24. **strength and ornament.** Though at this time Ireland was causing comparatively little trouble, Burke certainly exaggerates.

43 26. **mighty troubles.** The rebellions put down by Cromwell and William the Third.

43 32. **lucrative.** Used ironically.

43 34. **supply.** Revenue. Compare 50 4.

44 1. **Irish pensioners.** Government pensioners paid out of the Irish revenues.

44 7. **Henry the Third.** Fought with Wales, 1265-1267. See Green, I, 280-312.

44 8. **Edward the First.** Invaded Wales, 1277 and 1282. "The Statute of Wales which Edward promulgated at Ruddlan in 1284 proposed to introduce English law and the English administration of justice and government into Wales. But little came of the attempt; and it was not till the time of Henry the Eighth that the country was actually incorporated with England and represented in the English Parliament." Green, I, 334. See also *ibid.*, 324, 325.

44 12. **Lords Marchers.** Lords of the borders. From *march*, a boundary, or border. The English kings before Edward the First had granted to the lords such lands as they could win from the Welsh, and each lord executed the law in his territory. After the conquest, these lords retained their jurisdiction, though no new ones were created.

44 29. **proclamation.** "While providing for reinforcement to its army,

England enjoined the strictest watchfulness on its consuls and agents in every part of Europe to intercept all munitions of war destined for the colonies." Bancroft, IV, 129.

44 32. **disarm New England.** General Gage, acting under instructions from the home government, had made the attempt in the autumn of 1774. "He seized upon the ammunition and stores which were lodged in the provincial arsenal at Cambridge, and had them brought to Boston. He also at the same time seized upon the powder which was lodged in the magazines at Charlestown and some other places, being partly private property and partly provincial." *A. R.*, 1775, 18. General Gage's own account of the affair appears in a letter dated November 2, and laid before the House January 19, 1775. *P. H.*, 104.

44 34. **more hardship.** See 35 24, note.

45 6. **fisheries.** See 3 8, note. **foreign ports.** See 39 10, note.

45 8. **penal regulation.** In addition to the restrictions Burke mentions, no Welshman could buy land in a town or, with a few exceptions, hold a castle or fortress.

45 23. **laws made against a whole people.** Compare 33 23, note.

45 25. **twenty-seventh year.** 1535.

45 27. **rights of the crown.** "Wherefore the king's most royal majesty of mere droit and very right is very head, king, lord, and ruler." *Statutes of the Realm*, 1817, III, 563. Chapter 26 of 27 Henry the Eighth.

45 33. **fundamental security.** Compare 20 21–24.

46 6. **day-star.** Compare *II Peter*, i, 19: "Until the day dawn and the day-star arise in your hearts."

46 9. **Simul alba.** Horace, *Odes*, i, 12, 27–32: "When once their fair star has shone upon the mariner, the troubled water flows down from the rocks, the winds fall, the clouds flee away, and, since they [Castor and Pollux] have so willed, the threatening wave reposes on the deep."

46 15. **County Palatine.** A county in which the owner possessed royal rights, the same as those of the king in his palace. *Palatine* is from the Latin *palatium*, a palace. At the time referred to, Chester had its own courts, judges, and other such officers, and also a Parliament.

46 20. **Richard the Second.** Deposed for tyranny, 1399.

46 21. **archers.** About 2000 in number.

46 23. **petition.** The text, modernized in spelling, has been altered slightly from that of Dodsley in order to correspond to that of the *Statutes of the Realm*, 1817, III, 911. It forms part of chapter 13 of 34 and 35 Henry the Eighth. (Cook.)

46 24. **shewen.** An obsolete form.

46 26. **where.** Whereas.

46 29. knights. Members of Parliament representing a county. **bur gesses.** Members from boroughs.

46 31. disherisons. Deprivations.

46 33. commonwealth. Common welfare.

47 5. ne. Old form for *nor*.

47 14. libel. About the middle of June, 1774, the council of Massachusetts sent to Governor Gage, then recently appointed, an address reflecting severely on the policy of his two predecessors. Of this incident he says in a letter to the home government dated June 26: " The council sent me the enclosed libel on my predecessors in this government, in an address ; on which account I refused to receive it." *P. H.*, 86. According to the account in the *Annual Register*, 1775, 7 : " The address was rejected by the governor, who would not suffer the chairman of the committee to proceed any further, when he had read the part which reflected on his predecessors. He afterwards returned an answer to the council in writing, in which he informed them that he could not receive an address which contained indecent reflections on his predecessors, who had been tried and honorably acquitted by the Privy Council, and their conduct approved by the king; that he considered the address as an insult upon his Majesty and the lords of his Privy Council, and an affront to himself."

47 15. derogation. The argument that a petition questioning or denying the power of Parliament in any point should not be received, because it was a derogation from the rights of Parliament, was urged against the petitions from America. For instance, on March 14, 1769, the general assembly of New York offered a representation denying the right of Parliament to tax the colony. " Lord North opposed its being brought up, seeing they denied the right of the Parliament to tax them ; if they petitioned to remove any grievance, it was another thing; but Parliament having passed a law declaratory of its right to tax America, nothing should be received arraigning that right." *P. H.*, XVI, 604.

47 19. temperament. Tempering, or modification.

48 10. no way resembling. " And also by cause that the people of the same dominion have and do daily use a speech nothing like ne consonant to the natural mother tongue used within this realm." *Statutes of the Realm*, 1817, III, 563, chapter 26 of 27 Henry the Eighth.

48 12. Judge Barrington. Daines Barrington : born, 1727 ; appointed justice of the counties of Merioneth, Carnarvon, and Anglesey, all in Wales, 1757; died, 1800.

48 16. rebellion. See 35 23, note.

48 19. legislative authority is perfect. This argument had been urged again and again. For example, on February 6, during a discussion of the affairs in America, Solicitor-General Wedderburn said that "the clearest rights" of the legislative power were invaded and denied. *P. H.*, 233.

48 21. **virtually represented.** Another common argument. The following is a passage from the summary of the debates on the Stamp Act in 1766: "There can be no doubt but that the inhabitants of the colonies are as much represented in Parliament as the greatest part of the people of England are, among nine millions of whom there are eight who have no votes in electing members of Parliament. Every objection, therefore, to the dependency of the colonies upon Parliament, which arises to it upon the ground of representation, goes to the whole present Constitution of Great Britain. A member of Parliament chosen for any borough represents, not only the constituents and inhabitants of that particular place, but he represents the inhabitants of every other borough in Great Britain; he represents the city of London and all the other commons of the land, and the inhabitants of all the colonies and dominions of Great Britain, and is in duty and conscience bound to take care of their interests." *P. H.*, XVI, 201, 202. Cook notes that Dr. Johnson also, in *Taxation No Tyranny*, had written: "It must always be remembered that they [the Americans] are represented by the same virtual representation as the greater part of Englishmen; and that if by change of place they have less share in the legislature than is proportionate to their opulence, they by their removal gained that opulence, and had originally, and have now, their choice of a vote at home or riches at a distance." *Works*, VIII, 183.

49 2. **Opposuit natura.** Nature opposed. Juvenal, *Satires*, x, 152.

49 4. **meddle with no theory.** See 6 15, note.

49 6. **those who have been more confident.** In this number Franklin may be reckoned. In a letter to Governor Shirley February 22, 1754, he expressed approval of the plan. See Sparks's edition of Franklin, Boston, 1840, III, 64. But during his examination before the House of Commons January 28, 1766, he said that before the Stamp Act Pennsylvania, at least, had no desire for representation. *P. H.*, XVI, 158. Writing in 1769 he seems to have lost faith in the desirability of the plan. "It is in my opinion by no means impracticable to bring representatives conveniently from America to Great Britain; but I think the present mode of letting them govern themselves by their own assemblies much preferable." *Observations on Passages in "An Inquiry into the Nature and Causes of the Disputes between the British Colonies in America and their Mother Country."* Sparks's Franklin, IV, 283. (Cook.)

49 8. **arm . . . is not shortened.** Compare *Isaiah*, lix, 1: "The Lord's hand is not shortened, that it cannot save."

49 18. **Republic.** A sketch of an ideal commonwealth.

49 19. Utopia. A similar plan published in 1516 by Sir Thomas More, who lived 1478–1535. **Oceana.** Published in 1656 by James Harrington, who lived 1611–1677.

49 21. rude swain. Misquoted from Milton's *Comus*, 634, 635 : "*dull* swain."

49 22. clouted shoon. Furnished with clout-nails. See the *New English Dictionary*.

49 29. 1763. The beginning of the Grenville administration, which passed the Stamp Act.

49 31. grant. A voluntary contribution. See 57 9–14. **imposition.** A tax imposed.

49 33. legal competency. See 53 20–33, 54 1–7.

50 4. supply. See 43 34, note.

50 11. temple of British concord. An allusion to the Roman Temple of Concord. Compare 72 10–11.

50 24. fourteen. The government of Quebec and the thirteen colonies which formed the Union.

50 30. description. The parties named; that is, the colonies and plantations.

50 33. The second is like unto. Compare *Matthew*, xxii, 39: "And the second [commandment] is like unto it, Thou shalt love thy neighbor as thyself."

51 16. Non meus. Horace, *Satires*, ii, 2, 2, 3: "This is not my own doctrine, but that taught by Ofellus, a rustic, wise without rules."

51 20. rust that rather adorns. Compare Juvenal, *Satires*, xiii, 147–149 :

> Confer et hos, veteris qui tollunt grandia templi
> Pocula adorandae robiginis et populorum
> Dona vel antiquo positas a rege coronas.

"Compare also those who despoil some old temple of its massive chalices with their venerable rust, and the gifts of nations, or crowns dedicated by some ancient monarch." (Cook.) Burke had used the phrase "venerable rust" before. On November 27, 1770, in a debate on the power of the attorney-general, he said : "They have set before our eyes in every engaging light the respect and reverence which it [the power of the attorney-general] has derived from the savory mouldiness and the venerable rust of ages." *P. H.*, XVI, 1151. In another report of the speech Burke is made to say : "Several gentlemen have expressed a kind of superstitious reverence for the power of the attorney-general to file official informations, upon account of its supposed antiquity, as the father of Scriblerus venerated the rust and canker which exalted a brazen pot-lid into the shield of a hero.

I hope to scour off the false marks of antiquity which have made this power venerable, as effectually as the honest housewife scoured off the false honors of the pot-lid." *Ibid.*, 1190. The passage here referred to is from the *Memoirs of Martinus Scriblerus*, chapter iii: "Behold the shield. Behold this rust, or rather let me call it this precious *aerugo*, — behold this beautiful varnish of time, this venerable verdure of so many ages." Pope's *Works*, London, 1776, IV, 79. Possibly this passage rather than that from Juvenal suggested to Burke the phrase "venerable rust"; for, as the quotation at 32 33, 34 indicates, he seems to have been familiar with the *Scriblerus* papers.

51 22. **touch with a tool.** Compare *Exodus*, xx, 25: "And if thou wilt make me an altar of stone, thou shalt not build it of hewn stone; for if thou lift up thy tool upon it, thou hast polluted it."

51 27. **tracks of our forefathers.** The conservatism which appears so often in this speech runs throughout his work. Compare, "The old building stands well enough, though part Gothic, part Grecian, and part Chinese, until an attempt is made to square it into uniformity. Then it may come down upon our heads altogether, in much uniformity of ruin." *Present State of the Nation, W.*, I, 368. "Has he well considered what an immense operation any change in our Constitution is? how many discussions, parties, and passions it will necessarily excite? and when you open it to inquiry in one part, where the inquiry will stop?" *Ibid.*, 371. "The most dangerous of all principles, that of mending what is well." *Ibid.*, 421. "The dislike I feel to revolutions, the signals for which have so often been given from pulpits; the spirit of change that is gone abroad; the total contempt which prevails with you, and may come to prevail with us, of all ancient institutions, when set in opposition to a present sense of convenience or to the bent of present inclination; — all these considerations make it not unadvisable in my opinion to call back our attention to the true principles of our own domestic laws." *Reflections on the Revolution in France*, III, 264.

51 30. **wise beyond what was written.** Compare *I Corinthians*, iv, 6: "τὸ μὴ ὑπὲρ ὃ γέγραπται φρονεῖν." Authorized version: "That ye might learn in us not to think of men above that which is written." Revised version: "Ye might learn not to go beyond the things which are written." See also, "He is resolved not 'to be wise beyond what is written' in the legislative record and practice." *Appeal from the New to the Old Whigs, W.*, IV, 134.

51 31. **form of sound words.** Compare *II Timothy*, i, 13: "Hold fast the form of sound words."

52 13. **little in property.** Compare 28 5, note.

52 22. repealed. See 36 4, note. Compare, "About two years after this act [of 1767] passed, the ministry, I mean the present ministry, thought it expedient to repeal five of the duties and to leave . . . only the sixth standing." *Speech on American Taxation, W.,* II, 10.

52 23. regulating duties. A reference to what is called the Molasses Act, passed in 1733. For the provisions and the remonstrance, see 40 31, note. "The title of this act of George the Second . . . considers it merely as a regulation of trade : An act for the better securing the trade of his Majesty's sugar colonies in America." *Speech on American Taxation, W.,* II, 31.

52 28. duties of 1767. See 36 4, note ; 52 22, note.

52 30. Lord Hillsborough. Born, 1718 ; secretary of state for the colonies, 1768-1772 ; died, 1793. Though in general opposed to concessions to America, yet on May 13, 1769, he sent to the colonies a public circular letter from which Burke quotes the following passage in the *Speech on American Taxation, W.,* II, 20: "I can take upon me to assure you, notwithstanding insinuations to the contrary from men with factious and seditious views, that his Majesty's present administration have at no time entertained a design to propose to Parliament to lay any further taxes upon America for the purpose of raising a revenue ; and that it is at present their intention to propose the next session of Parliament to take off the duties upon glass, paper, and colors, upon consideration of such duties having been laid contrary to the true principles of commerce."

52 34. resolution of the noble lord. See 7 13, note ; 8 30, note.

53 8. representation in Parliament. See 28 19, note ; 49 6.

53 15. freemen. Those who have full rights of citizenship. **freeholders.** Those who possess absolutely or for life a piece of property.

53 24. passed the public offices. Approved by the proper authorities. In regard to the possible royal veto, see 36 22, note.

53 25. Those who have been pleased. An allusion to Grenville. "He was of opinion, which he has declared in this House an hundred times, that the colonies could not legally grant any revenue to the crown, and that infinite mischiefs would be the result of such a power." *Speech on American Taxation, W.,* II, 43.

53 30. some of the law servants. On February 10, 1766, during a debate in the Lords on the disturbances in America, Lord Chief Justice Mansfield argued that no money could be raised without the consent of Parliament ; for the agreement of any number of people to raise money for the king would be unconstitutional. By the Declaration of Right, pronouncing it illegal to levy money except by act of Parliament, all levies, said Mansfield, by "loan, gift, or benevolence " are void. *P. H.,* XVI, 174.

53 31. **if the crown could be responsible.** Whatever the English sovereign does officially is done by the advice of his ministers, who are held responsible.

54 3. **council.** A body of specially selected and sworn advisers of the king.

54 4. **first lords of trade.** A reference to a committee of the privy council having supervision of commerce and industry. See Introduction, xv. **attorney-general.** One of the chief legal advisers of the crown. **solicitor-general.** An officer associated with the attorney-general in the legal business of the crown.

54 17. **great expenses.** On January 28, 1766, Dr. Franklin testified to the House: "The colonies raised, paid, and clothed near 25,000 men during the last war [the French and Indian], a number equal to those sent from Britain, and far beyond their proportion. They went deeply into debt in doing this, and all their taxes and estates are mortgaged for many years to come for discharging that debt. . . . The sums reimbursed to them were by no means adequate to the expense they incurred beyond their proportion." *P. H.*, XVI, 153.

54 18. **so high.** So far back.

54 19. **1695.** During the long struggle between the French and the English colonists.

54 20. **1710.** The year of the successful expedition against Acadia, in which a number of New England troops took part.

54 24. **1748.** The year of the peace of Aix-la-Chapelle, the end of what is known as King George's War. England then restored to France Cape Breton, which had been colonized by the French but captured by the English.

55 1. **1756.** The time of the French and Indian War.

55 17–21. **Vol. XXVII.** The passages referred to are similar in phrasing to those quoted above.

56 4. **miserable stories.** In Franklin's testimony the following sentence occurs: "America has been greatly misrepresented and abused here in papers and pamphlets and speeches, as ungrateful and unreasonable and unjust, in having put this nation to immense expense for their defence and refusing to bear any part of that expense." *P. H.*, XVI, 152, 153.

56 5. **misguided people.** The English.

56 9. **paid no taxes.** An argument which appeared in nearly every debate on America. See, for example, the speech of the Duke of Grafton, February 10, 1766, when the repeal of the Stamp Act was proposed. *P. H.*, XVI, 165.

56 11. **Mr. Grenville.** George Grenville: born, 1712; prime minister, 1763–1765; died, 1770.

56 25. requisition. Note the distinction which Burke makes between money asked for and taxes imposed.   See 54 12.

57 17. utmost rights.   See 37 4, note.

58 2. An act for granting.   See 36 4, note.

58 4. drawback.   Rebate.   Duties collected upon the goods mentioned were partly or wholly repaid if the goods were again exported.

58 8. clandestine running.   Smuggling.

58 11. An act to discontinue.   See 36 4, note.

58 17. An act for the impartial administration.   See 36 4, note.

58 23. An act for the better regulating.   See 27 18, note.

58 27. An act for the trial.   See 35 24, note.

58 30. during the king's pleasure.   According to a clause of the bill, the decision as to reopening the port was to rest with the crown.   *P. H.,* XVII, 1165.

58 33. was not heard.   On March 14, 1774, during the debate on the bill, Mr. Dowdeswell asked if the House would not hear what Boston had to say in defence ; if the House would condemn without evidence in the absence of the parties.   *P. H.,* XVII, 1168.   **other towns.**   On March 25, Mr. Dowdeswell inquired : "What is the reason that you single out Boston for your particular resentment?   Have there been no other towns in America which have disobeyed your orders?   Has not Philadelphia, New York, and several other provinces sent back their tea?"   *Ibid.,* 1180.

58 35. Restraining Bill.   See 3 8, note.

59 9. less power.   In all the colonies, except Maryland, Connecticut, and Rhode Island, the crown had power of veto.   See Lecky, III, 324.

59 11. as great and as flagrant.   "A similar language was everywhere held ; or if there was any difference in the language, the measures that were adopted were everywhere directed to the same object."   *A. R.,* 1775, 13.   See 26 25, note.   The argument used against Boston was that it had been the ringleader in the disturbances.   "Boston has been the ringleader in all riots," said Lord North, when on March 14, 1774, he introduced the Boston Port Bill.   *P. H.,* XVII, 1165.

59 21. returning officer.   The officer who summoned the jury.   This duty was now put into the hands of the sheriff, who was appointed by the crown.   The object, of course, was to obtain juries favorable to the government.   See 27 18, note.

59 25. temporary.   The act was to continue in force three years after June 1, 1774.

60 10. during good behavior.   Bancroft thus relates an incident of the autumn of 1761 : "On the death of the chief justice of New York, his successor . . . was appointed at the king's pleasure, and not during good behavior, as had been done before. . . . The assembly held the new tenure of judicial power to be inconsistent with American liberty. . . . But in November the board of trade reported to the king against the tenure of good behavior as 'a pernicious proposition,' 'subversive of all true policy,' 'and tending to lessen the just dependence of the colonies upon . . . the mother country.' The representation found favor with the king ; and as the first fruits of the new system, on the ninth of December, 1761, the instruction went forth through Egremont to all colonial governors to grant no judicial commissions but during pleasure. . . . The assembly of New York rose up against the encroachment, deeming it a deliberate step toward despotic authority ; the standing instruction, they resolved, should be changed, or they would grant no salary whatever to the judges." II, 551, 552. (Cook.) "Hardy, governor of New Jersey, having violated his instructions by issuing a commission to the judges during good behavior, was promptly dismissed." *Ibid.*, 557.

60 18. **courts of admiralty.** "The jurisdiction of the courts of admiralty, which tried smuggling cases without a jury, was strengthened and enlarged, and all the officers of ships of war stationed on the coasts of America were made to take the custom house oaths and act as revenue officers." Lecky, III, 336. "The custom house and revenue officers, unlike other officials in America, were not paid by the local legislatures. They were appointed directly by the crown or by the governors." *Ibid.*, 328.

60 22. **more decent maintenance.** Since the judges were paid by fines imposed on goods that were condemned, there was a temptation to make large seizures. See Bancroft, II, 553. The original edition of the speech contains the following note : "The solicitor-general informed Mr. B. when the resolutions were separately moved, that the grievance of the judges partaking of the profits of the seizure had been redressed by office ; accordingly the resolution was amended." See 77 8.

60 32. **Congress complain.** In an address to the people of Great Britain issued by the Congress at Philadelphia, October 21, 1774, occurs this passage : "It was ordained that whenever offences should be committed in the colonies against particular acts imposing various duties and restrictions upon trade, the prosecutor might bring his action for the penalties in the courts of admiralty ; by which means the subject lost the advantage of being tried by an honest, uninfluenced jury of the vicinage, and was subjected to the sad necessity of being judged by a single man, a creature of the crown, and according to the course of law which exempts the prosecutor from the trouble of proving his accusation, and obliges the defendant either to evince his innocence or to suffer. To give this new

judicatory the greater importance, and as if with design to protect false accusers, it is further provided that the judge's certificate of their having been probable causes of seizure and prosecution shall protect the prosecutor from actions at common law for recovery of damages." *Journals of Congress*, I, 28.

61 13. **prove too much.** When the Stamp Act was repealed in 1766, thirty-four of the lords signed a protest, urging that if America pleaded lack of representation as a reason for disobeying the Stamp Act, the same reasoning extended " to all other laws of what nature soever, which that Parliament has enacted, or shall enact, to bind them in times to come, and must (if admitted) set them absolutely free from any obedience to the power of the British legislature." *P. H.*, XVI, 185.

61 25. **advocate for the sovereignty of Parliament.** During a speech of January 14, 1766, Mr. Grenville had said: " That this kingdom has the sovereign, the supreme legislative power over America, is granted. It cannot be denied ; and taxation is a part of that sovereign power. It is one branch of the legislation. It is, it has been exercised, over those who are not, who were never represented. It is exercised over the India Company, the merchants of London, the proprietors of the stocks, and over many great manufacturing towns. It was exercised over the palatinate of Chester and the bishopric of Durham, before they sent any representatives to Parliament. I appeal for proof to the preambles of the acts which gave them representatives : the one in the reign of Henry the Eighth, the other in that of Charles the Second." Mr. Grenville then quoted the acts and desired that they might be read. *P. H.*, XVI, 101.

61 28. **Lord Chatham.** The leading champion of America in Parliament. Born, 1708 ; though not nominally the prime minister, he was in fact head of the government, 1757–1761 ; died, 1778.

61 29. **in favor of his opinions.** Part of the speech of Lord Chatham, — then Mr. Pitt, — in reply to Mr. Grenville was as follows : " I come not here armed at all points with law cases and acts of Parliament, with the statute book doubled down in dog's-ears, to defend the cause of liberty ; if I had, I myself would have cited the two cases of Chester and Durham. I would have cited them to have shown that even under any arbitrary reigns Parliaments were ashamed of taxing people without their consent, and allowed them representatives. Why did the gentleman confine himself to Chester and Durham ? He might have taken a higher example in Wales, — Wales that never was taxed by Parliament till it was incorporated." *P. H.*, XVI, 104.

62 5. **de jure.** Legally. **de facto.** In fact.

62 27. **compromise and barter.** Burke is fond of applying this princi-

p*l*e in his arguments.   Compare, " Of one thing I am perfectly clear : that it is not by deciding the suit but by compromising the difference that peace can be restored or kept."   *Letter to the Sheriffs of Bristol, W.*, II, 231. " Men cannot enjoy the rights of an uncivil and of a civil state together. That he may obtain justice, he gives up his right of determining what it is in points the most essential to him.   That he may secure some liberty, he makes a surrender in trust of the whole of it."   *Reflections on the Revolution in France, W.*, III, 310.   " The rights of men in goverments are their advantages ; and these are often in balances between differences of good, — in compromises sometimes between good and evil, and sometimes between evil and evil."   *Ibid.*, 313.

62 33.   **communion and fellowship.**   From the *Book of Common Prayer* of the Church of England ; the beginning of the collect for All Saints' Day : " O Almighty God, who hast knit together thine elect in one communion and fellowship."

63 2.   **immediate jewel of his soul.**   Compare *Othello*, iii, 3, 155, 156 :

> Good name in man and woman, dear my lord,
> Is the immediate jewel of their souls.

" Our ruin will be disguised in profit, and the sale of a few wretched baubles will bribe a degenerate people to barter away the most precious jewel of their souls."   *Fourth Letter on a Regicide Peace, W.*, VI, 98.   **a great house is apt.**   Compare Juvenal, *Satires*, v, 66 : " Maxima quaeque domus servis est plena superbis," Every great house is full of haughty slaves.

63 11.   **improvement by disturbing.**   See 51 27, note.

63 16.   **cords of man.**   Compare *Hosea*, xi, 4 : " I drew them with cords of a man, with bands of love."

63 19.   **cautions us.**   Aristotle, *Ethics*, i, 3 : " It will be our endeavor to attain that accuracy which the nature of the subject admits ; for perfection is not required in all the labors of the mind any more than in all the works of the hand.   Political justice or virtue seems liable to this uncertainty. . . .   In matters so little stable we must be contented, therefore, with catching the general features of truth ; and our conclusions will deserve to be approved, if in most cases they are found to be useful and applicable ; for it is the part of wisdom to be satisfied in each subject with that kind of evidence which the nature of the subject allows ; it not being less absurd to require demonstrations from an orator than to be contented with probabilities from a mathematician."   Gillies's Translation, London, 1813, I, 242.

63 25.   **superintending legislature.**   See 34 2. note.

64 2. **unity of the empire.** On January 20, during the debate on Lord Chatham's motion to withdraw the troops from Boston, the Earl of Rochford held that the "unity of the empire should supersede every inferior consideration, because on that its prosperity, stability, and external grandeur immediately depended"; and he felt that any yielding would destroy this unity. *P. H.*, 166. In another debate of February 7, Lord Lyttelton "contended for the universality and unity of the British Empire." *Ibid.*, 276.

64 10. **separate.** The separate Parliament for Ireland was abolished in 1800. See Green, IV, 338.

64 24. **promised.** See 9 2–3.

64 25. **proposition.** See 7 13, note.

64 32. **having already debated.** See 8 8, note.

64 33. **before the committee.** When the whole house sat as a committee on the bill, February 20. *P. H.*, 319–338.

65 2. **mere project.** See 6 15, note.

65 6. **Experimentum in corpore vili.** Commonly, *Fiat experimentum in corpore vili*, Let us make the experiment on something worthless.

65 12. **antechamber of the noble lord.** In the cabinet or a committee of it.

65 15. **state auctioneer.** See 8 8, note.

65 27. **quarrelling.** See 8 5.

65 33. **complain.** See 36 22, note.

66 29. **composition.** Adjustment or agreement.

67 8. **English revenue.** England derived revenue from an import duty on tobacco, and also dealt largely in this commodity with foreign countries.

67 21. **confound the innocent.** When the Restraining Bill was proposed (see 3 8, note) the objection was at once raised by Mr. Dunning that New Hampshire, Rhode Island, and Connecticut ought not to be included in the punishment of Massachusetts. *P. H.*, 300. On February 28 a petition was presented from the Quakers, saying that on Nantucket about 4500 members of that sect, "entirely innocent in respect to the present disturbances in America," "would be exposed to all the hardships of famine." *Ibid.*, 383. On the same day a number of witnesses were examined, and Mr. David Barclay, agent for the committee of North American merchants, summed up the evidence as showing that "a great number of innocent subjects [would] undergo a punishment which they do not deserve, as by their occupation the majority of them are the most part of the year at sea, and consequently must have been absent from disturbances at home." *Ibid.*, 384. On March 6 "Mr. T. Townshend urged the cruelty and injustice of an act which made no discrimination between innocence

and guilt." *Ibid.*, 387. On March 15 the same evidence and on March 16 and 21 much the same arguments were offered in the Lords. *Ibid.*, 421–461.

68 2. **treasury extent.** A writ for valuing lands to satisfy a debt to the crown.

68 10. **quotas and contingents.** Apportioned to the several states.

68 17. **breaking the union.** See 7 13, note.

68 20. **their taste.** On the very day that Lord North introduced his so-called proposition for conciliating America, February 20, he said : " I agree, Sir, that it is very probable the propositions contained in this resolution may not be acceptable to the Americans in general." *P. H.*, 334.

68 32. **certain colonies only.** See 7 13, note.

69 4. **long discourse.** Three hours.

69 10. **mean to spare it.** Before the year 1775 closed, Burke must have spoken at least a dozen times more on America; and on November 16 he offered another bill for conciliating the colonies. *P. H.*, 963.

69 12. **steadily opposed.** In nearly every debate on American affairs Burke had spoken more or less at length in behalf of the colonies.

69 27. **Posita luditur arca.** The chest (that is, the whole fortune) is put up as a stake. Juvenal, *Satires,* i, 90. See 5 26, note.

69 31. **debt.** An evidence of the strength of the credit of the government.

70 29. **Ease would retract.** *Paradise Lost*, iv, 96, 97. Burke has substituted *retract* for the original *recant.*

70 33. **immense, ever-growing, eternal debt.** Compare *Paradise Lost*, iv, 52, "The debt immense of endless gratitude."

71 12. **return in loan.** "The Bengal famine of 1770 was followed by Lord North's Regulating Act, by which, in exchange for the loan of a million which the company required and the remission of the annual payment to the government of £400,000 a year, a new council was appointed by Parliament; a supreme court, of which the judges were appointed by the crown, was established ; and the governor of Bengal was made governor-general of India." Low and Pulling's *Dictionary of English History*, London, 1884, 398, 399. The reference was well calculated to appeal to Burke's listeners, because for the last five years Parliament had spent a great deal of time over the affairs of India and the East India Company. This powerful corporation was organized in 1600 and did not finally go out of existence till 1873.

71 17. **taxable objects.** See 67 8, note.

71 26. **enemies.** See 18 22, note.

71 34. **light as air.** Compare *Othello*, iii, 3, 322–324 :

> Trifles light as air
> **Are** to the jealous confirmations **strong**
> As proofs of holy writ.

links of iron.   Compare *Julius Caesar*, i, 3, 94, 95 :

> Nor airless dungeon nor strong links of iron
> Can be retentive to the strength of spirit.

72 2.   **grapple to you.**   Compare *Hamlet*, i, 3, 63 : "Grapple them to thy soul with hooks of steel."

72 10.   **sacred temple.**   See 50 10.

72 12.   **turn their faces.**   An allusion to a practice which the Jews, the "chosen race," observed of turning their faces toward Jerusalem to worship.   See *I Kings*, viii, 44, 45 : "If thy people go out to battle against their enemy, whithersoever thou shalt send them, and shall pray unto the Lord toward the city which thou hast chosen and toward the house that I have built for thy name, then hear thou in heaven their prayer and their supplication, and maintain their cause."

72 20.   **of price.**   Compare *Matthew*, xiii, 46 : "Who, when he had found one pearl of great price, went and sold all that he had and bought it."

72 28.   **sufferances.**   Permits.   **cockets.**   Sealed certificates that the duties have been paid on goods.

73 1.   **spirit.**   Compare *Aeneid*, vi, 726, 727 :

> Spiritus intus alit ; totamque infusa per artus,
> Mens agitat molem, et magno se corpore miscet.

> One common soul
> Inspires and feeds and animates the whole.
> This active mind infus'd through all the space
> Unites and mingles with the mighty mass.

> Dryden's Translation, 982–985.

73 6.   **Land Tax Act.**   An act annually passed for raising revenue.

73 9.   **Mutiny Bill.**   In order to keep the army under control of Parliament, two bills were passed annually : one for military supply, and the Mutiny Bill, providing for the trial of soldiers by military law.

73 17.   **profane herd.**   Compare Horace, *Odes*, iii, 1, 1 : "Odi profanum vulgus et arceo," I hate the profane herd and drive it from me.

73 25.   **all in all.**   Compare *I Corinthians*, xv, 28 : "That God may be all in all."

73 29.   **auspicate.**   To give a favorable turn to in commencing, — a sense derived from the Roman practice of taking the *auspicium*, or inspection of birds, before entering upon any important business.

73 31. **Sursum corda.** In the mass of the Church of Rome this phrase, or in the communion service of the Church of England the equivalent, " Lift up your hearts," is used just before the priest turns to the altar to consecrate the elements.

73 34. **high calling.** Compare *Philippians*, iii, 14 : "I press toward the mark for the prize of the high calling of God in Christ Jesus."

74 9. **quod felix.** May it be happy and prosperous.

74 17. **previous question.** The motion for closing debate.

INDEX.

———◆◆◆———

Paul W. Webb

implied repression
implied - notably
...le is an ... repression

1. Conditions alike
2. These four books were
   satisfied. and
   would ask for
   other reasons